Stuart Walker
    30 March 1984.
Magdalen College, Oxford.
        ———.

C000162822

THE 1945-1951
LABOUR GOVERNMENTS

Roger Eatwell
School of Humanities and Social Sciences
University of Bath

THE 1945~1951
LABOUR GOVERNMENTS

BATSFORD ACADEMIC

FOR MY PARENTS

First published 1979
© R. Eatwell 1979

ISBN 0 7134 0262 8 (cased)
    0 7134 0263 6 (limp)

Printed in Great Britain by
Billing & Sons, London, Guildford and Worcester
for the Publishers, B T Batsford Ltd,
4 Fitzhardinge Street, London, W1H 0AH

CONTENTS

ABBREVIATIONS

BBC	British Broadcasting Corporation
BMA	British Medical Association
GP	General Practitioner
ILP	Independent Labour Party
LRC	Labour Representation Committee
MFGB	Miners' Federation of Great Britain
MP	Member of Parliament
NATO	North Atlantic Treaty Organisation
NCB	National Coal Board
NEC	National Executive Committee
NHS	National Health Service
NUM	National Union of Miners
OEEC	Organisation for European Economic Cooperation
PLP	Parliamentary Labour Party
SDF	Social Democratic Federation
TGWU	Transport and General Workers' Union
TUC	Trades Union Congress
UN	United Nations
USA	United States of America
USSR	Union of Soviet and Socialist Republics

ACKNOWLEDGEMENTS

A large number of people have helped me while preparing this book (and previously while compiling my doctoral thesis on the Labour Party in the 1930s). I received helpful information from countless people who were politically active during the years described in this work, and for this I am grateful. I should like to thank those who gave me permission to see the private papers of the following: C.R. Attlee, A. Bevan, E. Bevin, the cabinet, G.D.H. Cole, Sir Stafford Cripps, Hugh Dalton, The Fabian Society, the Labour Party NEC, the Labour Spain Committee, Kingsley Martin, Mass Observation, the South Wales miners, R.R. Stokes, John Strachey, R.H. Tawney, Sir Charles Trevelyan, B. and S. Webb, and Dorothy Woodman. I am grateful to the library staffs at the University of Bath, and at the Bodleian, where most of the work on newspapers and less common secondary sources was done. Rodney Barker, of the London School of Economics, Colin Lawson, a colleague at Bath University, Michael Pinnock, an old Balliol friend, and Tony Wright, another Balliol friend, now at the University of Brimingham, read all, or parts, of early drafts and made valuable comments. Finally, but by no means least, I should like to thank my parents and Jane Bailey, who commented on style, and helped proof-read the manuscript.

INTRODUCTION

This book considers the record of the 1945-1951 Labour governments in a provocative and wide-ranging fashion. It is aimed primarily at the degree student of political history, but it has, I hope, something for a much wider audience, especially in the Labour Party and among socialists in general. It should also interest those who can remember the six turbulent years when Labour ruled Britain after the second world war. I cannot remember this era, as I was born during it. Nevertheless, I find the period a fascinating one.

In order to encourage the general reader to consult footnotes, I have only used them to refer to major secondary sources, and to make glosses on the text. I have tried to make reference in each section to the most important secondary sources. A short bibliographical essay at the end of this book also points out the most useful works. In both this section and references, I have tried to give the most recent publication date; I hope this will help readers to consult the most recent editions.

Since this is a political history, I have used basically a chronological approach for the central chapters covering 1945-1951. It has been impossible to consider in detail all aspects of the governments' record. Such a work would be of considerable length, and I have aimed at something relatively short. I have therefore concentrated on the main legislation and reforms introduced by Labour, though economic and, to a lesser extent, foreign, defence and colonial policies are not ignored. I have also provided an introductory chapter covering the road to 1945; in this I have tried to illustrate the main ideas and interests behind the formation of the party, Labour's eclipse of the Liberals, and the origins of the 1945 programme. In the final chapter I have set out my main conclusions about the achievements and failures of Labour's attempts to lay the foundations of the 'Socialist Commonwealth of Great Britain' promised in its 1945 manifesto, and contrasted them with some of the main conclusions reached by other writers.

My central contention is that although Labour implemented an extensive programme of reform during 1945-1951, in ideological terms its record is ambiguous. This ambiguity stemmed from many factors, but one basic problem was the nature of Labour's socialist vision. The Labour

Party has never been characterised by any single ideological tradition; its politics have in many ways been eclectic. Nevertheless, there have been strong general tendencies in the party, and especially in party policy. The most important of these has been Fabianism, with its commitment to a piecemeal, gradual movement towards public ownership within the existing Parliamentary-liberal democratic system, and efficiency-managerial ethic. 1945-1951 revealed serious problems in these beliefs: Labour's gradualism left the major centres of private power largely untouched, and its ethic in some ways resembled capitalism's commitment to production for private profit rather than private need, and to its hierarchical social structure. Trade union influence in the party also militated against a more inspiring conception of socialism; the unions tended to be narrow, and concerned with immediate issues such as employment and wages, again tendencies which in some ways reinforced capitalism's acquisitive ethic. Indeed, 1945-1951 indicated the need for Labour basically to rethink many of its central assumptions about the nature and achievement of socialism. Socialism encompasses many strands of thought, but central to most socialist doctrines has been a commitment to a society based on cooperation rather than competition; a society in which a high degree of economic and social equality is a major goal; a society in which collective needs are elevated above private ends! On such a definition, the 1945-1951 Labour governments' claims that they were socialist are debatable.

Chapter One

THE ROAD TO 1945

'clause 4 did not indicate . . . the presence of a coherent ideology. It is better regarded as a rallying point around which the adherents of different ideologies and representatives of different interests assembled.'

R. Harrison, 'The War Emergency Workers' National Committee, 1914-1920' in A. Briggs and J. Saville (editors), *Essays in Labour History, 1886-1923* (1971), p. 259.

Part one: Socialists, Trade Unionists and the Formation of the LRC, 1900

On 10 March 1900 the *Clarion*, the most popular socialist journal of the day, reported the formation of the infant Labour Party in the following words: 'At last there is a United Labour Party, or perhaps it would be safer to say, a little cloud, no bigger than a man's hand, which may grow into a United Labour Party.' These hopeful and yet cautious words reflect the sentiments of many sympathisers at the time. There was hope, for a united labour party had been a long time in coming. There was caution, for the new party was still clearly a 'little cloud', its unity was a distinctly uneasy one, and its purpose less than certain.

The inaugural conference of the Labour Representation Committee, as the Labour Party was known until 1906, was held in a dingy Memorial Hall near Ludgate Circus on 27-28 February 1900. The majority of the delegates present were working-class, representatives of trade unions, though there was a sprinkling of middle class among the members of the socialist organisations. Most of those who attended had few clear political ideas. They could agree on little except the need for separate working-class Parliamentary representation by men 'sympathetic with the aims and demands of the Labour movement'. The LRC adopted no wide-ranging programme; there was certainly no socialist commitment. To the extent that the party had an ideology it was one of labourism, a belief in the possibility of incremental change to the benefit of the 'labouring classes' within the existing framework of society, and particularly by Parliamentary means.[1] The LRC was a loose federal organisation, encompassing union and socialist bodies, which were represented at an annual conference and on an executive. Although initially far from all unions affiliated, from the outset they had a majority on the executive and a vast majority at conference. As the union leaders, and especially their members, were on the whole not socialists, the socialists were forced to subdue their desire for a socialist labour party.

The formation of the LRC stemmed directly from the activities and interests of two main groups — the trade unions and the socialist organisations.[2]

It is important not to put too much emphasis on the role of the socialists. Their membership was always small and they were badly divided, both internally and among themselves, though there were some similarities — for example, they tended to be insular. However, these organisations were not totally exclusive: there was some intermingling of ideas and cooperation, a tendency aided by the vagueness of many of their ideas. Moreover, the socialists advocated a more cooperative and equal society, they attacked a capitalist system which they identified with inequalities and production for profit rather than social need or responsibility. This helped provide a vision of a new world, and inspire a crusading zeal which did much to fire many of the activists who helped form the LRC. Finally, socialism allowed a caricature of the idle rich; denigration of capitalism and the bourgeoisie almost certainly had more popular appeal than some of the more empirical and theoretical presentations of socialism.

The first group to be formed in the late nineteenth century was the Social Democratic Federation, which emerged in 1884.[3] The SDF's supporters tended to be secular, heirs to the Enlightenment's suspicion of religion and mysticism. The SDF claimed that it purveyed Karl Marx's 'scientific' socialism, but its Marxism was confused, even non-Marxist. It believed in the so-called 'iron law of wages', a view which held that under capitalism trade unions could not alter significantly the financial position of the workers; such a view hardly helped recruitment among the growing number of unionists! More appealing was its support for the nationalisation of land, railways, mines, banks and all the 'means of production, distribution and exchange'. The SDF also believed in palliatives, in short-term ameliorative measures, such as the eight-hour day (at the time ten plus was common).

This support for palliatives was a factor in a major split which occurred in the SDF in 1884. Out of this schism arose the Socialist League. The

Socialist League also differed from the SDF in that most of its members rejected Parliamentary action. They were revolutionaries, though they tended to be vague about the origins and nature of this revolution. However, this vagueness did not help attract any significant number of members, nor prevent serious internal schisms. These factors played a part in the League's demise in the early 1890s (though its anarchist-communist tendencies lived on, and over a decade later helped inspire guild socialism). The SDF was therefore left alone on the British Marxist stage, briefly to play its part in the formation of the LRC, before its suspicion of trade unions led it back into a dogmatic and sterile isolation when it broke with the infant LRC in 1901.

Another group formed in the same year as the SDF was the Fabian Society.[4] The early Fabian Society was an eclectic organisation, containing constitutionalists and revolutionaries. However, from the late 1880s the group became increasingly associated with Parliamentarianism. This had much to do with the intellectual domination of Sidney Webb, a young civil servant who joined the Society in 1885.

Webb was an heir to a Darwinian and Spencerian evolutionism, to the belief that history showed that change could come peacefully. He espoused the Englightenment's empiricism; he stressed the importance of facts so that a case could be argued from expediency rather than principle; he believed facts alone could make socialists. Webb eschewed ethical proselytising, though like Comte, he believed in the possibility of moral regeneration among an administrative and managerial elite. In Webb's socialist vision there was to be no great transfer of power to the workers. The purpose was to make industry more efficient by gradually unifying control in the hands of the state or municipality. A unification of control would cut out wasteful competition and allow rational planning that would end capitalism's trade cycle; furthermore, state control would end over-charging by monopolies, and other restrictive practices. At the same time, the state would extend welfare provisions for the masses.

Webb's gradualist-managerialist-efficiency-welfare ideas attracted attention well outside socialist circles. Indeed, initially Webb believed in the permeation of the existing parties, a kind of political cuckoo principle. He held that the major parties were too strongly entrenched to be replaced easily. Moreover, like many of the SDF, he had little interest in the trade unions, believing them to be weak, narrow and divided. However, during the 1890s Webb, increasingly influenced by his wife Beatrice and others, began to despair of the Liberals as a collectivist organisation. At the same time, the Fabians became interested in the possibilities of the growing trade union movement. They therefore supported the formation of the LRC. Nevertheless, Webb and many of the Fabian Society viewed the formation of the LRC with serious doubts, still not certain that a separate labour party was needed, especially one tied so closely to the unions, and not committed to any form of socialism. It was an inauspicious beginning that hardly hinted at the domination which Fabian ideas were later to achieve in large sections of the Labour Party.

The last of the main socialist organisations to emerge in the late nineteenth century was the Independent Labour Party, formed in 1893.[5] The ILP was the heir to religious reformism in Britain, of the 'moral' or 'utopian' socialists, and their doctrines of cooperation and human brotherhood. However, a proposal to call the new party the 'Socialist Labour Party' was defeated at the inaugural conference, a reflection of the importance of the non-socialist group, and especially of the desire to appeal to general union and working-class opinion. The party's programme included a commitment to the collective ownership of the means of production, distribution and exchange, especially land, as well as to palliatives such as the eight-hour day. Nevertheless, the party's appeal was couched in millenarian terms, and its acceptance of the Parliamentary road revealed that it did not believe that the new kingdom was close at hand, nor that violence and class warfare would be necessary in the transition.

James Keir Hardie, the ILP's first President, was a devoutly religious man, a man who specifically sought the labour alliance — unity between socialists and unionists, who were far more numerous than the socialists and whose funds offered a promising source of finance. Hardie himself was until the early 1890s an active union leader, a recent convert to socialism, attracted by the lack of Liberal sympathy for trade union demands like the eight-hour day, and by his own failure to become Liberal Parliamentary candidate in the 1888 Mid Lanark by-election. In the same year he formed the Scottish Socialist Party, a party whose socialism, like that of its founder, was a distinctly vague form of ethical millenarianism. Four years later Hardie became the first working-class man to be elected to Parliament as an independent when he was returned for West Ham, a victory which did much to inspire the formation of the ILP. A decade later Hardie was to play a major role in persuading first the Scottish Trades Union Congress, and then the TUC itself, to convene the conference which met in the Memorial Hall in February 1900.[6] Hardie and the ILP therefore played an important role in attracting the unions to the banner of independent labour; moreover, their ethicalism and religious reformism were major factors in subsequently attracting support among an electorate that was swayed by strong emotional and religious preferences.

The fact that the LRC foundation conference took place only after the approval of the TUC had been achieved reflects the vital role which the unions played in the creation of the Labour Party. The TUC's decision in 1899 to convene the conference also indicates the major developments which had been taking place in the union movement. Although the growth of socialism within the unions explains part of these changes, it was not the major factor in explaining the 1899 decision.[7]

One major change in the late nineteenth century was the rise of un-skilled, general unions. These unions relied for their strength on the aggressive strike weapon; they were more militant than their craft fore-bears; they were more collectivist, stressing the existence of a labour movement. This development in turn helped promote the rise of employers' federations and attacks on trade unionism. In particular, a series of legal rulings in the 1890s removed many trade union rights, such as peaceful picketing. The unwillingness of the Liberals, or the Conservatives, to consider new legislation to rectify this situation seemed to point to the need for an independent working-class party, or at least a Parliamentary group which could hold the balance of power in the way that the Irish Party had done during 1885-1886.

It was hoped that an independent labour party would provide repre-sentation in the House of Commons, where, in the words of the LRC's first manifesto, 'the great battles between capital and labour are to be fought out'. If the socialists in general accepted Parliamentary action, the unionists were almost unanimous in their belief that change could come via existing institutions, though of course many in the unions did not seek an especially radical change.

Part two: The Eclipse of the Liberals, 1900-1931

In the 1900 general election the majority of the working-class vote went to the Liberals; only two LRC candidates were returned. In the 1906 and 1910 elections Labour's representation rose to twenty-nine, forty and then forty-two seats, but in 1914 the Liberals remained the largest party in Parliament, and the main party of the working class. Moreover, the rise in the number of Labour seats owed much to a pact with the Liberals; as Labour began to adopt a more independent position after 1910 it even began to lose seats. Some commentators, notably P.F. Clarke and Trevor Wilson, have argued that the decline of the Liberals was not a necessary one.[8] However, in reality a combination of economic, social and political developments doomed the Liberal Party to eclipse.

In the late nineteenth century a series of factors threatened the Liberals' appeal to the working class. First was the growth of class consciousness. Secondly, powerful interests in the party, notably the industrialists, saw the rise of the new unions as a threat to their position, and an unacceptable distortion of the free market. Thirdly, many of the middle-class Liberals who dominated most local caucuses were loath to select working-class men as Parliamentary candidates. Fourthly, there was a growing tension in the party between the old *laissez faire* Liberalism, and newer, more collectivist and state interventionist ideas. Finally, there were signs of a decline of nonconformism, the religion of much of the working class, and closely associated with Liberalism.[9]

None of these factors necessarily doomed the Liberals. The class consciousness was certainly not socialist; growing trade union consciousness might be a better description. The industrialists in the party may have left, as landed wealth had largely already done. Not all working-class people wanted working-class MPs; the Liberal leadership was also trying to encourage working-class candidatures. Many working-class people had strong *laissez faire* views; and in the long run it was not certain that the Liberals were incapable of becoming a more collectivist and interventionist party. Finally, nonconformism was essentially an individualist doctrine; while its decline in one sense threatened the Liberals, in another it opened the way for a new appeal.

However, these factors were to have important effects on many of those who helped form the LRC. And the establishment of the Labour Party in turn was to make it more difficult for the Liberals to retain and build on their working-class support. In particular, the rise of class consciousness, and the decline of nonconformism and religion in general, opened the way for a labour and socialist party. Voting in the late nineteenth century involved strong religious allegiances, class was an incidental rather than determining factor; economic interest was not a major perspective. As religion declined, the way was opened for a new ethical appeal along socialist lines that often played upon existing religious values; at the same time, growing class consciousness helped a specifically labour party. For the Liberals to have survived, it would have been necessary to find a new emotional-ethical appeal, a difficult task for the party of Gladstone. The Liberals would also have had to appeal along class lines. The contradictions within the party, the presence of a strong Conservative Party, and the emergence of the Labour Party combined to make this impossible.

In the 1906 general election the Liberals won a landslide victory, and during 1906-1910 enacted a major programme of social reform, a programme in part designed to appeal to working-class opinion. However, a constitutional crisis with the Lords in 1909 led to two closely fought elections in 1910. The Irish Party once again held the balance of power, and Home Rule returned as a major issue. The Liberals after 1910 were also plagued by the women's suffrage movement's militancy. There was growing industrial strife and working-class militancy; an inflationary situation, which saw real wages fall between 1900 and 1914, helped spread syndicalist, guild socialist and radical ideas. A worsening international situation also came increasingly to dominate the scene. Nevertheless, writers like Clarke have overstated, or mis-stated, the problems which the Liberals faced at this time. It is certainly wrong to imply that these years destroyed the Liberal Party. Domestic reform was not neglected during this period; the fact that there was not more reform, or greater changes in the Liberal Party, reflects the tensions and divisions in the party, rather than a party distracted by other issues.

Writers like Wilson are right to point to the problems which the first world war posed for the Liberals, but these problems had already been plaguing them, and the main effect of the war was to hasten the Liberal decline. During the war religion suffered a further shattering blow; the nonconformist revival of the early twentieth century, a major factor in the 1906 landslide, had been followed by a rapid wane; during the war nonconformism disappeared as a significant political force in most areas. In the early stages of the war the Liberals faced the misfortune of being in government at a time when much greater interventionism was necessary to fight a war that had already alienated many in the party. During the war the Liberals split between the followers of Lloyd George and those of the party's leader, Asquith. Although national unity engendered by the war helped hide the extent of the break, it was a serious one, reflecting more than just ambition. It was a split over policy, over the older versus the more collectivist and interventionist Liberalism.

The Labour Party also split during the war, but this tended to help the party. Before the war, foreign policy was not a major concern for Labour, especially among its union members, though even among the socialists there had been little interest. Labour's policy, to the extent that it had one, was a vague internationalism, tinged with pacifism. After the outbreak of war, the pacifists and those opposed to the war, like Ramsay MacDonald, helped give the party a radical front and created a bridge with those Liberals who were appalled that the 'party of peace' should have led Britain into war. But others in the party who were strongly nationalist, or hostile to German militarism, supported the war. Men like Arthur Henderson, who succeeded MacDonald as Chairman of the party when the latter resigned over his attitude to the war, found themselves increasingly consulted by the government and even given office, a fillip to Labour's self-confidence and respectability. The federal organisation of the party, and its sense of the existence of a labour movement also meant that an essential unity remained through the many divisions of the first world war. Moreover, as the main split in the party was over its attitude to the war and government, there were not too many troubles in reuniting at the end of the war.

This was not the case for the Liberals, and the Liberal schism was carried into the 1918 general election when Lloyd George, who had succeeded Asquith as Prime Minister in 1916, fought with his Liberal supporters in a coalition which won a landslide victory. Asquith was left to fight with the rump Liberals, who went down to a humiliating defeat. Labour ran 361 candidates, a massive increase on 1910, gained 20.8 per cent of the poll and 57 seats. Labour had become the largest opposition group only eighteen years after its foundation.

The Liberal split undoubtedly helped Labour. However, even if the Liberals had fought as a united party, Labour would have improved significantly on its pre-war position. Already before 1914 there were signs that Labour was beginning to be able to stand on its own two feet; although Labour lost some seats during 1910-1914, it was showing an increasing independence of the Liberals and building its own organisation. During the war further developments helped Labour. The growth of trade union influence, the expansion of the state's role, the increasing spread of socialist ideas and religious decline — these and other factors are not easy to document or quantify, but it is wrong to ignore them. Moreover, 1918 saw a new Reform Act, and with it the final enfranchisement of all men, all married women, and single women over thirty (1929 was the first general election in which the 'flappers' had the vote).[10]

The working-class members of this new electorate had no traditional loyalty to the Liberals; class was the most likely determinant of their voting pattern. The Labour Party was the natural beneficiary, though the Conservatives may have done well from the new women voters; certainly before 1918 Liberal leaders had feared that the women's vote would help the Conservatives. The Liberals had previously been the main party of the working class, and class was increasingly becoming an issue in elections before 1918,[11] but in part the connection was a religious and historical one, which provided no reason for the Liberals to retain and build on this support in a very different post-war world.

To the extent that class was not a determinant in 1918, the Conservatives and Labour had certain advantages over the Liberals. The Liberals' appeal was in many ways a rational one, and this in a world which seemed to have passed by the party's traditional rational concerns, while the Liberals' more emotive and ethical links with the nonconformists were also being undermined by a general decline in religious practice. The rational aspects of Conservative and Labour thought seemed more suited to the twentieth century. Their emotive and ethical elements had more staying power: the Conservatives stressed issues like nationalism, and played on deference; Labour caricatured the rich, promised a new world of brotherhood and prosperity, in which social need and responsibility rather than profit would be the guiding aim — in which socialism would be the ruling order.

1918 was important to the Labour Party not only because of the general election of that year. Earlier in 1918 Labour had adopted a new constitution, defining its organisational structure and including the famous Clause IV, committing the party 'To secure for the producers by hand or by brain the full fruits of their industry and the most equitable distribution thereof that may be possible, upon the basis of the Common Ownership of the Means of Production and the best obtainable system of popular administration and control of each industry and service.' (Distribution and exchange were added in 1929.)

Clause IV was almost certainly the work of Sidney Webb. The war had helped underpin Webbian socialism, with its emphasis on institutional, state action; during the war he had been the intellectually dominant figure on the main Labour coordinating body. By 1918 he believed that a socialist commitment was necessary for the Labour Party to appeal to an increasingly socialist electorate.[12] The senseless, bloody slaughter of a 'capitalist' war, and the success of the October 1917 Russian revolution fuelled the fires upon which socialism fed. Clause IV sought to attract this growing body to the Labour Party. Clause IV helped differentiate Labour from the Liberals, an important factor in view of the ending of the electoral agreement which had helped Labour in the 1906 and 1910 elections. Clause IV set Labour apart, but was in many ways vague; it invited all, it was a red lamp which promised everything, and yet nothing.

1918 further saw the Labour Party adopt a new programme, drafted by Webb, called *Labour and the New Social Order*. Although this document owed much to Webb and Fabianism, it is wrong to see it, in Ralph

Miliband's words, as a 'Fabian blueprint'.[13] The emphasis on efficiency and welfare was clearly Fabian. Its piecemeal Parliamentarianism was a reflection of what Webb was to call at the 1920 Labour conference 'the inevitability of gradualness', though the specific proposals for nation-isation owed more to union pressures. Its lack of emphasis on the ethical side of socialism revealed a strong Fabian tendency, which was shared by many in the union leadership. The absence of reference to municipalisation reflected an eye to union desires: the unions were collectivist and national, with little interest in such ideas. More generally, the programme was clearly embryonic and vague, even contradictory. Here was no precise Fabian document. Like Clause IV, it was a red lamp which attracted socialist political myths.[14]

The man who most helped foster this mythology was MacDonald.[15] As party Secretary during 1900-1912 and Chairman during 1912-1914, he had been Labour's most prolific writer and speaker. In his early days MacDonald had been a Liberal, and aspects of his later thought con-tained strong elements of radical Liberalism, for example his discussion of limits of individual freedom and state action. MacDonald's socialism involved no conflict within society; he saw society as an organism and spoke of the attainment of socialism in evolutionary terms. He rejected class analysis and warfare, preaching a socialist version of national unity. In this line of argument MacDonald had much in common with Webb and others, but MacDonald's socialism was vague. In part this revealed MacDonald's intellectual inability to sustain and develop an argument. However, it also reflected an awareness that the labour and socialist movement was divided, that if Labour was to become a mass party it needed an all-embracing ideology, one which would appeal to the emotions and the masses as well as to the intellect and the few. Here was not some academic engaged in theoretical debate, or producing a practical plan; here was a man engaged in building a mass Labour Party, a point missed by many critics at the time and since.[16]

Labour's acceptance of Clause IV and adoption of a new programme in 1918 therefore has to be treated cautiously. It is wrong to argue, as commentators like Samuel Beer have done, that these developments made the party comprehensively socialist.[17] This argument ignores the continuing diversity of opinion within the party, and the presence, especi-ally in the unions, of many who cannot be called socialist in any sense of the word. Moreover, Labour's 'socialist' commitment was a vague one; it committed the party to few specific policies. This is an important point to bear in mind when considering the record of the 1924 and 1929-1931 minority Labour governments.

In the 1922 general election Labour won 142 of the 414 seats it contested, and increased its poll to 29.7 per cent. The 1922 Parliament was
to be a short-lived one, for in 1923 the Conservative leader, Baldwin,
decided to call an election on the issue of tariff reform. Conservative
support for protection had been a major factor in the 1906 Liberal landslide, and in 1923 the old cry of free trade helped publicly to reunite the
Liberals, but in private the divisions remained. In spite of Liberal reunifi-
cation, Labour still kept in front, capturing 191 of the 427 seats it contested, and 30.7 per cent of the poll. When Parliament reassembled Asquith
decided to vote with Labour against the Conservative government, believing
that a short period of minority Labour government would burst the
party's bubble. It was a decision that was to backfire badly, though those
like Maurice Cowling who have argued that the Liberals at this time could
still have survived ignore the underlying factors behind Labour's rise.[18]

MacDonald, who had been re-elected Chairman of the party in 1922,
chose a Cabinet that reflected a clear desire to impress on moderates
Labour's respectability, although it also revealed a shortage of talent
in a PLP which, while less dominated by aged union-sponsored MPs
since the 1922 election,[19] was still a somewhat unimpressive group.
Subsequently, MacDonald, who doubled as Foreign Secretary, pursued a
widely admired conciliatory and relatively internationalist policy, which
further helped attract Liberals. Other ministers also clearly courted the
Liberal vote. Undoubtedly the 1924 election was a disastrous one for the
Liberals, who emerged with only a quarter of the seats they had won in
1923. Labour continued its progress, winning 151 of the 514 seats it
contested; while this meant a loss of seats, its percentage of the poll at
33.3 continued to rise.

In spite of the increased number of votes which Labour won, 1924
represented in some ways a setback for Parliamentary socialism. The
record of the government provided an easy target for critics on the left,
especially in the newly formed Communist Party of Great Britain. Growing
support for direct action was undoubtedly a factor behind the TUC's
decision in May 1926 to call a general strike in support of the coal miners'
resistance to wage cuts. However, writers like Miliband who have argued
that the considerable support for the strike proves the existence of mass
radicalism ignore the fact that there was almost certainly a connection
between the moderate nature of the call and the response.[20] Throughout
the strike both the political and union Labour leadership maintained a
cautious position. David Coates has argued that the Labour leadership in

the 1920s was becoming increasingly moderate under the influence of the 'Parliamentary embrace', and desire for office.[21] Certainly Labour leaders feared that extremism during the strike might cost the party votes, but the leadership had never been radical in any extreme sense.

The speedy collapse of the strike resolved fears that it might harm Labour. Indeed, in the 1929 general election Labour emerged for the first time as the largest party, capturing 287 of the 596 seats it contested, and 37.1 per cent of the vote. Even so, Labour had again failed to win an outright majority, and MacDonald therefore formed his second minority administration. In 1928 Labour had issued a new programme entitled *Labour and the Nation*. This included some specific commitments, but the programme left much vague, especially on the major issue of the day — unemployment. MacDonald's government proved incapable of curing the problem; the Chancellor of the Exchequer, Philip Snowden, could only conceive Bank of England and Treasury conventional palliatives; Jimmy Thomas, the minister specifically responsible for tackling unemployment, was overwhelmed by the problem.

In 1931 the Conservative and Liberal parties demanded an enquiry into 'economies' to balance the budget (the Liberals who, Coates has argued, were more radical than Labour on the basis of their 1929 programme,[22] were still badly divided and in general moderate). When the committee reported it recommended cuts, most of which fell on the already pitifully low rate of unemployment benefit. This was followed by increasing pressure on the pound, and foreign bankers demanded that further loans be tied to retrenchment. The Cabinet agreed to some cuts, but at this point the TUC intervened and refused to accept any cut in unemployment benefit.[23]

Shortly after, MacDonald announced that he was to form a National Government. Few Labour members joined him in this venture, although those who did included Snowden and Thomas. MacDonald and the defectors were branded as traitors, and expelled from the party. When MacDonald subsequently led the National Government into a general election, his place in Labour demonology was assured. The result of the 1931 general election was one of the greatest reversals in British electoral history. The National Government swept the board. Labour won only 52 of the 516 seats it contested, although its vote at 30.8 per cent remained more constant. Nevertheless, in spite of the disasters which had afflicted Labour, the Liberals had disappeared as a serious independent force. Labour had definitely become the second party in the land.

Part three: The Emergence of a Programme, 1931-1945

Some, notably Miliband, have seen the events of 1931 as having no significant effect on the Labour Party. Others have seen them as leading to a socialist rebirth. There is an element of truth in both views, though each is essentially misleading; the Labour Party remained a complex coalition, and generalisation is difficult.[24]

The events of 1931 were rapidly to become as much a tale from party mythology as from party history. There was a serious point behind each of the myths, but they tended to divert attention from the central problems in the party's policy. Labour's dependence on Liberal support, and the limitations which this was supposed to have imposed, led mainly to a belief that there should be no more minority governments. The belief that the government had been broken by a 'bankers' ramp' did not lead to a questioning of the basic tenets of gradualism, but rather to a reinforcement of the desire to control the Bank of England. The defection of MacDonald was not seen as the culmination of Labour's failure, but more as an act of gross betrayal, an act that indicated the need for stricter controls on the leader by the PLP, and on the PLP by the NEC and conference. Finally, the belief that election smears (for example, that a Labour government would raid Post Office savings to pay unemployment benefit) had panicked people into voting for the National Government, reinforced the increasingly heard argument that Labour could only secure full and lasting power by appealing on a moderate programme.

In reality, Labour's failure lay more in the government's inability throughout its period of office to deal with the stagnation of the old staple industries, the worsening trade balance and growing unemployment. For many in the Labour Party socialism was an ill-defined ideal to be realised sometime in the indefinite future, and embodied in the Fabian doctrine of the inevitability of gradualness. It was a doctrine which held that although capitalism was inefficient and prone to slumps, there would be no cataclysmic collapse. Instead, there would be a slow transition to socialism via the existing Parliamentary institutions, and a gradual acquisition of power by the state. In this essentially millenarian and passive conception of socialism is to be found Labour's central governing problem: it was committed to working through Parliament to replace an inefficient and unstable capitalism, but had no definite policies as to how this should be done. The collapse of the Labour government in 1931 had not proved the futility of trying to work through Parliament; it had simply shown that mythology and rhetoric were not enough for a governing party.

There were some in the party who were not carried away by the mythology, especially on the left. In 1932 the increasingly Marxist ILP voted to disaffiliate from the Labour Party, slipping quickly into oblivion. Many in the ILP preferred to remain within the Labour Party, and some from this group helped form in 1932 a new organisation – the Socialist League, a name which recalled the small socialist group of the late nineteenth century. The League launched a major assault on the nature of Labour policy, preaching a quasi-Marxist class-based radicalism. The League's sterile dogmatism had little appeal outside a minority of activists, and in 1937 it was disaffiliated for persistent disloyalty.[25] However, the League raised some important questions – questions which can be seen most clearly by considering the ideas of its leader after 1933, the messianic Sir Stafford Cripps, who had been Solicitor General in 1931, and a moderate!

Cripps derived many of his ideas from G.D.H. Cole and Harold Laski. They saw 1931 as the symbolic end of the complacent gradualist and millenarian tradition. They sought to convert Labour to a new, and more aggressive, gradualism. They argued that changes would be necessary in legislative procedure, particularly the abolition of the House of Lords and the use of emergency legislation, so that a future Labour government could act speedily. They sought to define a clear programme. Cole especially after 1931 wrote prolifically on the question of a new Labour programme, and the relationship between gradualism and the private economy. In particular, he argued that without control over the central financial institutions it would be impossible to ensure a stable and prosperous economy during the transition to socialism. Cole claimed that without such a policy Labour was caught in a dichotomy. A prosperous economy was made unlikely by the disruptive and disincentive aspects of a government seeking to use tax and interventionist measures for social purposes; in an economic crisis a Labour government would be in trouble because revenues would be low and its ability to undertake reform limited.[26] Whilst rejecting the old piecemeal, complacent approach Cole therefore remained true to much of Fabianism, especially in its institutional emphasis, and the playing down of the ethical side of socialism – interesting developments in view of Cole's earlier guild socialist position.

Cripps never fully appreciated Cole's economic arguments, preferring a crude quasi-Marxist belief in the imminent collapse of capitalism. However, he accepted much of Cole and Laski's critique, and certainly held their view that a more radical policy would attract support rather than lose it. Cripps often presented his ideas in a fashion that helped alienate support. Nevertheless, this should not cloud the fact that he tried to raise in the party serious questions concerning Labour's socialism, a point frequently ignored by critics at the time and since.[27] Also, although Cripps was personally aloof, his radical socialist vision was capable of arousing great enthusiasm among audiences. Cripps had entered politics relatively late in life, having come to believe that through politics God's work could best be done; he spoke with the fervour of the religiously inspired. Alone among the Labour leaders of the 1930s, he could regularly pack the largest halls. But essentially Cripps was a paradox; in some ways he represented the new, post-1931 ideas, yet his blend of rationality, vagueness and ethicalism was very much part of Labour's older style.

The majority of the Labour leadership did not accept this left-wing critique. The left in general was divided, and many on the left, like Cripps, were prone to sterile sloganising, and lack of tactical sense. These factors helped obscure the more serious aspects of the left's case. Some Labour intellectuals, like Hugh Dalton, the Under Secretary for Foreign Affairs during 1929-1931 and a university lecturer in economics, believed that the left's case grossly exaggerated the opposition a future Labour government was likely to meet.[28] He further thought that part of the left's plans resembled dictatorship a little too closely, especially in a world in which democracy seemed threatened. There was certainly a widespread feeling in the leadership that such left-wing 'extremism' would lose votes. This was particularly true of Herbert Morrison, who had been Minister of Transport during 1929-1931.[29]

Nevertheless, there was a general acceptance that the existing Labour programme left much to be desired; as R.H. Tawney, the third of the major inter-war Labour theorists, noted: existing Labour programmes would nationalise land, mines and banking in one sentence, and abolish fox-hunting in the next.[30] Clement Attlee, the Postmaster General in 1931, was typical of many when he called for a clearer policy, with more detailed priorities.[31] To help remedy this situation the NEC in December 1931 set up a Policy Sub Committee.

'Planning' quickly became the keyword. The concept of planning was now a new one. It may be found in the 1918 Labour programme, and in earlier documents. Many in the party had become interested in the idea after the inauguration of the first Soviet five year plan in 1928; indeed, the Russian 'revelation' was arguably a greater influence on the party than the Russian revolution. Its impact can be seen in extreme form in the case of the Webbs. After 1931 they became disillusioned with a Labour Party dominated by 'non-scientific' trade unionists. They turned to the rational-technocratic promise of the new god which had arisen in the east. In *Soviet Communism: a New Civilisation?*, published in 1935 (and reprinted two years later without the question mark), they expressed their devotion. In Russia's system they found their spiritual home, and became archetypal rational fellow travellers.[32] Most in the Labour Party did not travel so far, but planning became an important aspect in Labour thinking. However, the Policy Sub Committee's planning gave little thought to the question of the nature of the socialist ideal, or how the transition from a capitalist to a socialist society would take place. Planning seemed to mean mainly the channelling of funds into the depressed areas within a basically capitalist framework, a conception which was strongly attacked at the 1933 Labour conference.

At the 1932 conference there had been considerable criticism of other policy statements. Indeed, the reports on the nationalisation of the electricity and transport industries were withdrawn, because of attacks on the absence of provision for trade union nomination to the boards. Also, an amendment to the report on banking which committed the party to nationalise the joint stock banks was narrowly carried against opposition from the platform. However, these decisions should not be seen as involving the rejection of the public corporation form of nationalisation, practised by Morrison during 1929-1931 in setting up the London Passenger Transport Board. Nor did it mean the adoption of a more aggressive gradualism. In the first instance, withdrawal resulted mainly from the demands of one of the major unions, whose General Secretary had no love for Morrison; and what was sought in no way approached workers' control. The vote on the joint stock banks in part reflected the currency of the 'bankers' ramp' interpretation of the events of 1931. Nor should too much be read into a resolution, passed without a vote, stating that the 'main objective' of the party was the establishment of socialism. The decision which the NEC took in May 1933 rejecting suggestions that the party should change its name to 'Socialist' or 'Labour and Socialist' reflects more than just the traditionalism and sense of the past in the Labour Party. It reflects the essential continuity after 1931 of the moderate and gradualist attitudes of most of the leadership.

This continuity can be seen in the two Labour programmes issued in the 1930s. The 1934 programme, *For Socialism and Peace*, was more detailed than any previous statement. But among its contents was the rather ambiguous claim that 'for the most part' nothing short of public ownership and control would be necessary for banking and credit, transport, electricity, water, iron and steel, coal, gas, agriculture, textiles, shipping, ship-building and engineering. Moreover, it adopted none of the radical critiques which emerged after 1931 from the left, other than nationalising the banks; and on the exact nature of socialist planning and society it remained vague. Also, although drafted by Tawney, it showed few signs of his ethical critique of capitalism. These points were even more true of the 1937 *Immediate Programme*, which dropped the commitment to nationalise the banks, cotton, and iron and steel — mainly as a result of trade union lack, or loss, of interest in these policies.

In no section of the party was the continuity of leadership and policy more clear than within the trade unions. During the 1920s the unions had lost some of their influence within the party. The attitude of the Labour leaders, union preoccupation with their own concerns, the leftward swing in some unions before the general strike, and the 1927 Trade Disputes and Trade Unions Act, which dramatically reduced Labour's income from the trade unions — these and other factors helped separate the union and political leadership. The events of 1931 more than reversed this trend, though the dwindling of support for direct action, reflected in the 1928 Mond-Turner talks on union-management conciliation, and subsequent discussion of joint consultation, helped pave the way. After 1931 there was a conscious determination on the part of several union leaders, notably Ernest Bevin, the General Secretary of the TGWU, and Walter Citrine, the Secretary of the TUC General Council, to re-assert a more thoroughgoing control.[33]

The history of the Labour Party for the remainder of the 1930s can only be understood against a background of the aftermath of 1931, for the years 1932-1939 were to see mounting anger on the Labour left, and increasing hostility of the non-trade union wing of the party towards the union leadership.[34] At the same time, the union leadership became increasingly angered by what it saw as the intellectualism (a term of great abuse) and disloyalty (a term of even greater abuse) of elements on the left, and by the tendency of the political leadership in general to devote more and more time to issues which were not of immediate concern to the unions, notably foreign policy.

Foreign policy plagued Labour as the 1930s progressed. The absence of any serious discussion of foreign policy in the past, the pacifist tendencies in sections of the party, and suspicions of the government made it difficult to formulate a policy in the face of the rise of fascism beyond a vague internationalism, which masked a strong nationalism in sections

of the party, especially the unions.[35] Foreign policy also diverted attention from the field of domestic policy. This was an understandable
tendency in view of the rise of fascism, Japanese aggression, and the highly
emotive Spanish civil war, which ended in 1939 with General Franco's
defeat of the republic, but it meant that vital questions about the nature
of Labour's socialism were pushed further into the background. Finally,
foreign policy increasingly became the main area of division in the party,
notably when a section in the late 1930s came out in favour of a popular
front against the National Government, and its much criticised foreign
policy — the appeasement of the fascist powers.

In the 1935 general election Labour gained 38.1 per cent of the vote,
more than ever before, but it won only 154 of the 552 seats it contested.
It was therefore clear that Labour alone could not challenge the government, and the popular front sought a united opposition, both in Parliament and in the country. The movement was a communist tactic, but it
gathered considerable support, and might have gained much more had
the Labour Party supported it. However, the majority of the Labour
leadership was totally opposed to cooperation with the communists, or
for that matter anyone else. The union leadership in particular opposed
such cooperation, both on ideological grounds, and fearing that it might
threaten their power within the party. The tactic was rejected as unworkable, and branded a communist manoeuvre (always a useful way of
damning any policy opposed by the leadership). As a result, Cripps was
expelled from the party in January 1939 for persistent disloyalty in
advocating the tactic. Subsequently, Aneurin Bevan, who was rapidly
emerging as a leading figure on the left, and many others were expelled.[36]

Nevertheless, the popular front in the longer run helped promote a
short-term consensus within the party, and paved the way to 1945. A
popular front would have involved running a basically capitalist economy.
This led many on the left to re-examine the possibility of a healthy capitalism, and helped promote interest in J.M. Keynes's *General Theory*, first
published in 1936 (a factor ignored by those such as Paul Addison who
have sought to present the impact of Keynes and the road to 1945 in more
deep-rooted consensual terms[37]). The ground for Keynes had been prepared to some extent by the American New Deal, and more theoretically
by the under-consumptionist economics of J.A. Hobson; indeed, Cole
was to claim snidely that Keynes simply 'sugar-coated' the Hobsonian
doctrine in a language difficult enough for economists to study it seriously.
This interest in Keynes was of great importance to Labour's subsequent
unity, for many of the more moderate members of the party came to see

in Keynes a theoretical basis for their piecemeal gradualist, even mixed-market positions. In particular, his theories seemed to promise a prosperous capitalism in which interventionism was a stabilising rather than destabilising influence. In most cases Keynesianism did not convert the Labour left to a more moderate position, although the best known British Marxist theorist of the 1930s, John Strachey, began his movement back to moderation as a result of the *General Theory*.[38] The point is rather that Keynes helped make the left aware of the possibilities of a moderate short-term programme, and helped undermine some of its arguments of the early 1930s — or at least appeared to do so.

Nevertheless, in the summer of 1939 the Labour Party was still badly divided. By-elections and opinion polls indicated that it was heading for its third general election defeat in a row. There were increasing attacks on the low-key leadership of Attlee, whose self-effacing style had helped in his selection over the more assertive Morrison in 1935; 'And a little mouse shall lead them!' Dalton wrote cattishly in his diary. Criticism was especially strong in the unions, who felt that the political leadership was not paying sufficient attention to their interests. In March 1939 Bevin, the union leader most interested in foreign policy, wrote to the NEC complaining about the party's preoccupation with this area. David Howell has written that 'Labour, after 1931, was not a trade union-dominated party',[39] but the union leadership expected close compliance by the political leadership, and over the summer of 1939 there was considerable talk in the smoke-filled rooms of the need for industrial leadership of the party, talk that cannot be dismissed simply as idle gossip or plotting.

The outbreak of war effectively solved these problems. During 1940, as Britain stood alone against fascism, a deep sense of national unity developed, a feeling fostered by extensive wartime propaganda. Increasingly as the war continued this propaganda was to change in theme from one of survival to the new Britain which would be created at the end of the war. This in turn helped create a climate of opinion conducive to a reforming party. Within the Labour Party there was a strong desire to use the war as an opportunity to popularise Labour's themes of economic and social change, and in 1941 the NEC set up a Committee on Post-War Economic and Social Reconstruction. The TUC similarly saw a great opportunity for pushing reform, though the union leaders in general saw the war domestically more as an opportunity to achieve greater consultation within industry and with the government. There was especially strong rank-and-file support for using the war as an opportunity to push radical policies.[40]

At the 1944 Labour conference, pressure from the floor led to the adoption of a more radical programme than had been proposed by the NEC. Many on the left supported such a policy not just for doctrinaire reasons; people such as Bevan, who had been readmitted to the party in late 1939, rejected the moderate electoral strategy, believing that a more radical programme would gain votes, that Labour should fight on a class 'we versus them' appeal. The NEC's programme had included no measure of nationalisation, other than the Bank of England — a far more moderate programme than proposed by the TUC. The revised programme included 'the transfer to public ownership of the land, large-scale building, heavy industry, and all forms of banking, transport and fuel and power', and demanded the passing of 'Appropriate legislation to ensure that the national assets, services and industries shall be democratically controlled and operated in the national interest, with representation of the workers engaged therein and of consumers.'

The pressure for a radical policy caused the Labour leadership some problems, and not only for electoral and ideological reasons. Shortly after the outbreak of war the major parties had agreed to an electoral truce, which many Conservatives took to mean a political truce. This Conservative attitude became important when in May 1940 the Labour Party agreed to the formation of a coalition government under Winston Churchill, a government which included Attlee, Bevin, Morrison, Dalton and several other Labour leaders. Attlee, and especially Bevin, largely accepted Churchill's desire to play down domestic issues, a desire which in part reflected a belief in the need to maintain the coalition for the duration of the war, and the fact that social reform was a highly sensitive issue, not least among the many Conservative backwoodsmen.

An excellent example of the problems this created came after the publication of the Beveridge Report in December 1942. The report recommended a new universal social insurance scheme, a national health system, and other social reforms. Although there were some fears in the Labour Party that Sir William Beveridge, a prominent Liberal, might steal Labour's progressive clothing, and there were more serious doubts about the ideological foundations of the proposals, the Beveridge Report attracted widespread support in the party, and among the public. However, the Labour members of the government agreed not to push for a positive acceptance of the report. The result was considerable recrimination, and a backbench revolt.

Nevertheless, in the longer run this tension almost certainly helped the Labour Party. The presence of Attlee, Bevin, Morrison, Dalton and others in the government gave the Labour leaders experience of public office, and probably more publicity than if they had remained in opposition. The price of participation — a moratorium on public pressure for reform — amounted to little, for in practice the government was the most reformist since 1905-1914. Meanwhile, outside the government members of the Labour Party pressed strongly for further reforms; the Labour Party therefore became associated with proposals for a new Britain. This tendency was further encouraged by the fact that it was mainly Labour members of the government who concerned themselves with domestic policy, which was hardly surprising as some of the proposals were more detailed versions of earlier Labour policies.

It is arguable that towards the end of the war Labour could have broken the electoral truce, even forced a general election. Many in the party, especially Bevan and the left, after 1942 sought this. However, by-election victories would have done little for Labour, and a general election in wartime would have presented many, though not insuperable, problems. The Labour Party may also have lost support for appearing to have provoked an election. Respect for the Labour leaders as a result of their wartime office may not have been as strong in 1943 or 1944 as it was to be after the successful conclusion of the war against Germany in 1945. More importantly, in 1943 and 1944 Labour had not finalised its programme for the next election, though this in part was a result of the lack of desire on the part of the leadership for an early election. *Let Us Face the Future*, the new manifesto, did not appear until April 1945. It was on this manifesto that Labour fought the 1945 general election.

Chapter Two

THE 1945 GENERAL ELECTION

'Politically, the undoubted leftward swing is essentially away from old beliefs, not yet clearly or enthusiastically directed towards a new source.'

Mass Observation post mortem on the 1945 general election. Mass Observation Papers, file report 2282.

Part one: The Background, Campaign and Results

The end of the European war brought the deteriorating situation within the Churchill coalition to a head. On 11 May Churchill met Bevin and Morrison. He claimed that the Conservative Party was keen on a July election, but pressed for a continuation of the coalition until after the defeat of Japan. Morrison wanted an October election: he felt that this would give sufficient time for parties to make their preparations, and by October a new electoral register would be in operation. Bevin was tempted by the idea of continuing the coalition, as was Attlee after his return from the founding conference of the United Nations.[1] Churchill's arguments were reinforced by the fact that many Labour leaders were doubtful about Labour's chances in a general election.

However, when the Labour NEC considered Churchill's proposals only three members supported the continuation of the coalition. It was not clear how long the Japanese war would last, and there was mounting pressure from all sections of the party, particularly the left, to hold an early election. In a letter to Churchill on 21 May Attlee pointed out that there were acute differences between the parties, especially over economic policy. Churchill's suggestion of a referendum to test public opinion on the issue was rejected as alien to the British political system. Attlee therefore proposed an autumn election, claiming that July smacked of Conservative self-interest.

Churchill replied by tendering his resignation to the King. Four hours later he was summoned back and asked to form a new administration. He accepted the commission, and asked for a dissolution of Parliament, which was granted. Britain would go to the polls on 5 July for the first time in a general election since November 1935.[2]

The electoral campaigns and programmes of the Conservatives and National Liberals, who provided most of the ministers in the new government, were to all intents and purposes the same. The Conservatives had no detailed policy, and the National Liberals were in the same position.

The Conservative manifesto for the 1945 general election was appropriately titled *Mr. Churchill's Declaration of Policy to the Electors*. Among the contents on the domestic front were: an acceptance of government responsibility for maintaining 'high and stable levels of employment'; the recognition of house building as the most important task, with the promise to control the prices of building materials, to continue rent controls, and to plan the use of land; a commitment to introduce a compulsory National Insurance Scheme; and the establishment of a 'comprehensive health service'. These policies were presented in a somewhat vague fashion, and coexisted uneasily with more general attacks on planning and government intervention (though there has always been some tension in Conservative ideology between its more libertarian and collectivist aspects). These proposals also followed sections in the manifesto dealing with foreign policy, the Empire, Commonwealth, and defence.

Foreign policy figured prominently in the Conservative campaign generally, with the Conservatives promising to maintain Britain as a major power, and to preserve the Empire and Commonwealth. The Conservative campaign concentrated on Churchill, whose campaign was a characteristically combative one. In particular, he issued a series of 'smears' against the Labour Party. A Labour government would introduce a *Gestapo*; it would be controlled by the NEC, the Chairman of which was the left-wing Laski, who on 15 June issued a statement saying that Attlee should not be bound by any decisions reached at the Potsdam peace conference until they had been discussed by the party. This statement, and Labour's constitution, gave the latter charge some plausibility, but the first smear had no justification. Indeed, it is hard to comprehend in view of the lack of extremism among the Labour leadership, and the policies presented in the 1945 Labour manifesto.

This was entitled *Let Us Face the Future*. Revealingly, foreign policy came at the end, whereas it had come at the beginning of the Conservative manifesto. In many ways Labour's policy in this sphere was similar to the Tories'. The main difference was a greater emphasis on post-war international cooperation, and a promise of 'the advancement of India to responsible self-government'. Domestic policy was the dominant concern.

The manifesto stated that 'The Labour Party is a Socialist Party, and proud of it. Its ultimate purpose at home is the establishment of the Socialist Commonwealth of Great Britain — free, democratic, efficient, progressive, public-spirited, its material resources organised in the service of the British people.' But, in keeping with the party's gradualist tradition, it was argued that 'Socialism cannot come overnight.' The manifesto therefore put forward a specific programme for a Labour government.

Labour's programme in 1945 was both an extension of the past, and something new. The playing down of the ethical side of socialism, the gradualism, the commitment to the Parliamentary road, the emphasis on efficiency rather than redistribution of power in economic policy, the acceptance of fair compensation for the owners of industries brought under state control, the absence of any serious commitment to workers' control even in nationalised industries — these were very much part of Labour's past. So was the acceptance of individual freedoms in certain spheres, such as worship and speech, yet the unwillingness to tolerate the 'freedom to exploit others'. But at the same time, *Let Us Face the Future* was far more detailed than any previous manifesto, and included some measures which had not figured in earlier such documents. This can be seen from a comparison with Labour's previous short statement of policy, the 1937 *Immediate Programme*.

The 1937 programme promised nationalisation in four main fields — finance, transport, coal and power; it also included an ambiguous reference to land. All these were included in the 1945 programme, though the reference to land was again unclear; additionally, there was a commitment to nationalise iron and steel, added to the list because of a revival of interest in the main union involved, its inclusion in the 1944 TUC Interim Report on Post-War Reconstruction, and demands at the 1944 Labour conference for more nationalisation. The *Immediate Programme* was distinctly vague on unemployment and social policy. It promised a 'determined attack on insecurity due to fear of unemployment', and aid for the depressed areas; it promised to raise social benefits and that 'Health Services' would 'be extended'. *Let Us Face the Future* was far more specific and wide-ranging. It promised full employment, stressing the need for government intervention in the economy and various controls: the effects of a quasi-Keynesian optimism are clear. It committed Labour to press 'rapidly with legislation extending social insurance over the necessary wide field to all'. It also promised a National Health Service, a major house-building programme, price controls and other policies. For these, and other reasons it is wrong to argue, as Miliband has done, that the

1945 programme was 'no advance' on the 1937 statement.[3]

Even so, it is important not to overstate the differences. Certainly many on the left were disappointed with the document, particularly after the left-wing successes at the 1944 Labour conference. At the 1945 conference, held in May, there were several criticisms of *Let Us Face the Future*, especially over foreign policy and the nature and extent of nationalisation. Nevertheless, the conference saw little trouble from the left. While Labour's policies in many areas were hardly new, even similar to those of other parties, they were presented as part of a general movement towards socialism. Moreover, the announcement of a dissolution during the conference further helped produce a closing of ranks for the coming struggle.

The Labour campaign, closely reflecting the policies put forward in *Let Us Face the Future*, stressed domestic policy and post-war reconstruction, though it was in many ways backward-looking.

The analogy with the first world war, and Lloyd George's failure to build 'homes for heroes' who had suffered so much in the trenches, figured prominently in Labour's campaign. Bevan had set the tone for this theme in his book *Why Not Trust the Tories?*, published in the previous year. This book bitterly attacked the failure of the inter-war Conservative Party in the face of mass unemployment and misery, an attack echoed by many others during the election. John Strachey, who had been reconciled with Labour during the war, listed the troubles of the inter-war years in the 1944 edition of his famous *Why You Should Be a Socialist*, and added that under socialism real wages would be at least ten times as much!

The inter-war years further featured as a sub-theme in the Labour campaign in the argument that the Conservative appeasement policy in the 1930s had helped cause the second world war. This was an extension of a theme developed in books like *Guilty Men*, written by a young Michael Foot and friends as early as 1940, and by many Labour speakers during the war. Labour may have tacitly accepted Churchill's claim to being the man who won the war, but it constantly sought to drive a wedge between him and the party which, it was alleged, had left Britain woefully unprepared for a conflict which it had helped cause.

Therefore although Labour's campaign was far more programmatic than any previous one, especially before 1935, mythology was not completely eliminated. Some socialist rhetoric remained, and the attacks on the Conservatives in the inter-war years helped foster new myths. The inter-war years were years of prosperity in many areas, of new semidetacheds, of baby Austins; the Labour record on foreign and defence policies in the 1930s also left much to be desired. The Labour Party had few ideas about how to cure unemployment, especially before the mid-1930s; and there were some defences of the National Government's appeasement policy. But many in the Labour Party, for example Bevan and Foot, were not engaged in an academic discussion of these years. They were propagandists, they were intent on creating new myths that would produce an anti-Conservative consciousness, that could be easily understood. In its mythical methodology, the Labour campaign in 1945 retained strong links with earlier campaigns, though the myths in 1945 tended to be more anti-Tory than pro-Labour.

Labour during the election campaign, in keeping with its position since 1918, refused any form of electoral agreement with other parties. The Labour campaign stressed that the Labour Party was the only serious alternative to the National coalition. The Labour leadership was undoubtedly worried by a possible fragmentation of the progressive vote. By-elections since 1942 had been showing remarkable swings away from the Conservatives, but the electoral truce meant that these swings were not to Labour candidates, and it was not clear what would happen now the truce had ended. Opinion polls gave Labour a clear lead during 1943-1945, but opinion polls were being used for the first time in a general election, and they were not widely trusted. Certainly the Labour leaders had little faith in them.

Similarly, the Liberal leaders took little notice of the polls, claiming they would make large gains. The Liberals, exploiting the Beveridge Report to the full, put forward a quite radical programme of their own, and 306 candidates, including Beveridge (compared to the National coalition's 618 and Labour's 603). The communists put up 21 candidates and played heavily on public admiration for the Red Army's exploits. Common Wealth, a new radical party formed in 1942, put forward 23 candidates, although none of these were in seats where Labour was running a candidate.

Political pundits and Conservative leaders predicted a Conservative majority of up to 100 seats. The result, which was declared on 26 July to allow the service votes to be collected, could hardly have been more different. The Conservatives had suffered their greatest reverse since the Liberal landslide of 1906. Labour had won 166 seats from the Conservatives, and lost none of them. Labour had gained a total of 393 seats and 48.0 per cent of the poll, compared to 154 seats and 38.1 per cent in 1935. The National coalition won only 210 seats, and 39.6 per cent of the poll, compared to 429 seats and 53.3 per cent in the previous election.

The Liberals held 12 seats and 9.0 per cent of the poll, compared to 21 seats and 6.8 per cent in 1935 (achieved by only 161 candidates). The communists won 2 seats, their electoral apogee, and 0.4 per cent of the vote, compared to 1 and 0.1 per cent in 1935 (achieved by 2 candidates). The turnout at 72.7 per cent was 1.7 per cent higher than in 1935. The swing to Labour was 11.8 per cent, and Labour was left with an overall majority of 147[4]

Part two: Analysis of the Results

Labour had won for a large number of reasons. It is important not to impute to the electorate anything approaching total knowledge of party programme, or rationality. However, Labour's victory should not be seen as an accident, or analysed in simplistic swing-of-the-pendulum terms. The use of opinion polls for the first time in a general election means that there is a more concrete basis for analysis than existed for any previous election, though this is not to deny that polls pose serious methodological problems, especially the idiosyncratic Mass Observation.[5]

Margaret Cole has argued that Labour was helped by a long-term development of education, and emergence of a literate population, open to new appeals.[6] However, though education may have helped spread the socialist gospel, it also spread conventional values; the average schoolboy almost certainly entered the adult world with an ingrained social conservatism, and sense of warmth over the large red areas on his school atlas — red, the colour of imperialism, not socialism. Almost certainly more important were two other long term factors. First, the growth of class consciousness since the late nineteenth century was bound to help a specifically labour party, although not necessarily produce socialists. Secondly, the electorate changes over time; increasingly an electorate was emerging which had been socialised in a less deferential climate, which could not remember a time when the Liberals were a power in the land. Certainly opinion polls showed the importance of class in voting, and the appeal of Labour to the young.

The inter-war years also helped Labour. Mass Observation found that Lloyd George's failure to build a land fit for heroes played on the memories of many, though it is an overstatement to claim, as A.J.P. Taylor has done, that 'Lloyd George brought ruin to Churchill from the grave.' More importantly, for most of the inter-war years a Conservative, or Conservative dominated National Government, held office. It was therefore easy to identify the Conservatives with the mass unemployment of these years, with the hated dole and the means test, with a system that elevated profit above people. This was hardly a past which people wished to conserve, particularly in areas of former high unemployment, where Labour did well in 1945. Even in areas where unemployment had been lower, the fear of unemployment often remained strong. The Conservatives' rejection of collective security, and cooperation with the Soviet Union, further helped Labour's claims that it was the party more likely to keep the peace after 1945, that Labour was the party of principle rather than blind nationalism, that in future left would understand left (a phrase first used by Bevin at the 1945 conference to refer to French socialists, but widely taken to refer to the USSR).

The war itself aided Labour in many ways, though it is important not to overstate the role of the war, as writers like Arthur Marwick have done.[8] It was during the war that opinion polls came to give Labour a lead. In 1938, when polls first began sounding political opinion in Britain, and 1939 Labour never seemed in a position to win a general election; after 1942 polls gave Labour a comfortable lead.

It has been argued that the participation of Labour leaders in Churchill's government helped make them better known to the public, and demonstrated their administrative competence. Attlee's self-effacing style further helped emphasise the team aspect of the Labour leadership, whereas Churchill's more self-assertive style stressed his separation from colleagues and party, a factor which helped Labour's attempts to drive a wedge between Churchill and the Conservatives. Mass Observation found that shortly before the election four of the top six politicians mentioned by people were Labour, with Churchill first, but Attlee and Bevin second and third (Morrison was fifth and Cripps, who rejoined Labour in early 1945, sixth).[9]

There is more serious evidence that wartime propaganda, particularly after 1942, was a major factor in Labour's victory. In the early years of the war propaganda for domestic consumption simply stressed survival and social unity; it usually had little to do with political and social development, though there were notable exceptions, like the Boulting brothers' short 1940 film, *Dawn Guard*, in which a young Home Guarder tells his older colleague of the need to create a new Britain after the war. Increasingly after 1942 propaganda began to stress this new Britain which would come at the end of the war. The theme of reconstruction and social reform, pushed so forcefully after the publication of the Beveridge Report, could only help Labour. The 'fair shares' campaign to make people accept rationing had clear egalitarian implications. Certainly Mass

Observation found high levels of social unity, a desire for change, and growing egalitarianism. These changes should not simply be attributed to propaganda, but the use of film and radio especially helped the message reach large audiences.

Non-government propaganda during the war also pointed to the evils of British society in the inter-war years, and stressed the need to create a new Britain. The evacuation of many poor people from the inner cities at the beginning of the war produced a social revelation for many — children and mothers, louse-ridden, incredulous that the space under beds could be wasted. These horrors were widely reported. The need for the creation of a new Britain was pressed strongly in the mass circulation *Picture Post*, the *Daily Mirror*, and many other newspapers, which in general were less partisan than in peacetime; indeed, reformist tendencies earned *The Times* the somewhat undeserved label of 'the threepenny edition of the *Daily Worker*'. Pamphlets, periodicals and books were used to push similar themes. The Left Book Club, formed in 1936, had long been doing this, and some have attributed to it a major role in preparing the way for Labour's victory in 1945.[10]

However, it is important to see this propaganda in perspective. Extensive propaganda, especially in a pluralist society, does not guarantee mass conversion; if anything it tends more to crystallise and reinforce existing opinions and tendencies.[11] In view of this, it is reasonable to doubt the extent to which it produced socialists in any serious sense of the word, especially as much of the propaganda was compatible with moderate reformism. If anything, the propaganda served more to reinforce Labour's attacks on the record of the inter-war Conservatives. Reformist and socialist propaganda also had to be seen against a counter-cultural background, and one in this case which stressed strong traditional values. For example, the majority of literature produced during the war, let alone read, had far from socialist implications or values.

There are similar problems in assessing the extent, and impact of religious revival during the war. It would be easy to overstate the trend, or the extent to which it favoured the left rather than the right. Nevertheless, religion almost certainly helped reinforce an ethical approach to politics, which should have aided Labour. Moreover, in 1942 William Temple was appointed Archbishop of Canterbury. This socialist primate of the Church of England proved a prolific Christian-socialist proselytiser during the war.

Many have claimed that during the war left-wing propaganda was disseminated within the army by the Army Bureau of Current Affairs.[12] The existence of left-wing leanings among the forces is confirmed by

Mass Observation's work, but Mass Observation also found high levels of apathy and cynicism in the forces. The exact breakdown of the service vote is not known, though for reasons of age, class and sex alone it should have been largely Labour. However, it is known that only 59.4 per cent of those in the services entitled to vote did so. It is also interesting to note that the Labour Party's Secretary in his report to the NEC on the election did not see this vote as a socialist one, claiming that it was predominantly Labour, but largely 'ignorant'.

The extension of government controls over the economy during the war played into Labour's hands by emphasising the possibility of considerable interventionism, and giving Labour the task of defending what in many ways had become the *status quo*. Similarly, the war promoted interest in the Soviet Union, and aspects of its system such as planning. Although the origins of an intellectual interest in planning can be traced back to the first Soviet five year plan in 1928, and beyond, the war undoubtedly furthered the *dirigiste* climate of opinion which had been gathering support — and not just in left circles — for many years.[13]

These wartime economic changes were accompanied by full employment and significant increases in real wages among workers, though many in the armed forces did less well. Wage rates in 1944 stood at 143 compared to 100 in 1939; prices on the working-class index stood at 201 compared to 158 (1914=100); but as a result of considerable overtime, earnings rose to almost double the rate of inflation.[14] Rationing, taxation and other policies meant that the average standard living was that of a pre-war artisan, and controls made this average a reasonably meaningful figure (though a black market helped the rich). So real increases in earnings were not always translated into consumption. Nevertheless, people in general were better off.

Finally, during the war the Conservatives allowed their organisation to run down, a factor later stressed by them in explaining their defeat.[15] Labour too did the same, especially in the early years of the war. But by 1945 the organisations of the parties were probably nearer in efficiency than at any previous election, and the normal massive Conservative advantage in cars to carry voters to the poll (admittedly sometimes crafty Labour ones) was further undermined by a shortage of petrol.

Some factors may have had an effect in the run up to the election, although the most frequently cited aspects indicate a trend in the opposite direction to the movement of opinion shown in polls. In May, Gallup gave Labour a lead of 16 per cent, but by the end of the campaign this was down to 6 per cent. This seems to emphasise that Labour's victory has to be understood mainly in the medium and long run, although both parties picked up support in the polls during the campaign, which indicates a gathering of support from 'don't knows' and supporters of other parties, especially Liberals without a candidate to vote for.

The Conservative campaign centred very much on Churchill, and some aspects of this campaign have been criticised.[16] Churchill's emphasis on foreign affairs reflected an interest not shared by many in the electorate. Mass Observation found that Churchill's statesman-like position was undermined by his smear attacks, which revived memories of earlier 'stunts', like the Post Office savings scare in 1931 — memories reinforced by the Labour campaign. These smears contrasted sharply with Attlee's calm dignity. Opinion polls also found that some who admired Churchill as a war leader doubted his fitness to lead in peacetime, remembering earlier events, such as his inflammatory role during the general strike in 1926. Even so, for all the failings of his campaign, and bitter memories in some working-class areas, it seems unquestionable that the Conservatives would have done worse without Churchill.

Many have stressed the advantages of Labour's manifesto and campaign over the Conservatives'. In particular, Labour emphasised the issues which opinion polls found that people believed to be important, especially housing, which was thought the most important issue by 41 per cent of the electorate, and full employment, thought most important by 15 per cent. The Conservatives pressed these themes as well, and it would be wrong to believe that the campaigns, or people's conceptions of them, were simply socialism versus *laissez faire*. But Labour's proposals were more specific, and the party did not have a long governmental record to defend.[17]

Some Conservatives were later to claim that the mass media, notably the BBC, helped Labour. For the first time, in 1945 radio figured prominently in a general election campaign. In his report on the election, the Labour Secretary claimed of radio that 'To an important degree it countered press hostility.' The Conservatives claimed that radio was biased against them, probably remembering the vague social democratic sentiments of popular wartime broadcasters, like J.B. Priestley. However, in general it is more accurate to remember that radio during the campaign was very cautious in terms of politics. The press in 1945 was more pro-Labour than ever before, notably as a result of support from the *Daily Mirror*, which gave Labour a second mass circulation daily to go with the semi-official *Daily Herald*. In 1945 the circulation of the national dailies which supported the two major parties were for the first time almost equal, though the Conservatives retained a large lead in other branches of the press. Even so, it is doubtful if this helped Labour much during the election campaign. Most people read papers with similar political complexions to their own; it is also dubious to what extent people read the political content. The media's impact was undoubtedly greater in the long run, especially in its reformist agenda-setting during the war.[18]

A final point concerns the electoral system. Overall it distorted Labour's position, giving it 61.0 per cent of the seats for only 48.0 per cent of the vote (in 1935 it gave Labour 25.4 per cent for 38.1 per cent of the poll). More specifically, the movement of population since the last major redistribution in 1918 meant that the average Labour seat was smaller than the average Conservative one (and had become more so since 1935). This more than made up for the fact that Labour had more seats with large majorities, and was worth twenty to thirty seats to Labour. Population movements during the war, especially evacuation, also probably helped Labour by taking working-class people from seats with large Labour majorities, though it is not clear how many registered in the new constituencies. On the other hand, the out-of-date register and low service vote would have worked against Labour; plural voting additionally must have given Labour's opponents a small number of extra votes. More importantly, the fact that the Liberals did not contest all seats helped the Conservatives more than Labour, as opinion polls indicated that Liberals were more likely to vote Tory than Labour; but the increase in Liberal candidates compared to 1935 would have taken more votes from the Conservatives.

So, what were the most important factors in Labour's historic landslide victory in 1945? How should the result be analysed?

One common approach has been to see the results in terms of the social composition of Labour's vote.[19] Mass Observation argued that among 1935 voters there was only a small net swing to Labour, indicating considerable support for Labour in 1945 from the young (and 1935 non-voters). Similarly, Labour had a distinct lead among male voters, especially trade unionists. But the evidence for the frequently held view that Labour won in 1945 because it attracted an increased middle-class vote has to be treated with care. Labour won many seats with large middle-class populations. Polls showed that Labour received 21 per cent of the middle-class vote, almost certainly more than ever before, though well below the Conservatives' 54 per cent. One reason for this seems to have been a reforming idealism of a section of the middle class, especially the educated and those in non-productive employment; some middle-class people also expected to do well under Labour's promised welfare-managerial-efficiency rule. But many middle-class Labour voters were upwardly socially mobile as a result of the growth of the middle class: that is they were often working class by origin, and sometimes continued to self-identify as such, with important voting implications.[20]

It is vital to remember that Labour won more working-class votes than ever before, and in total these working-class gains were larger than the middle-class ones. Opinion polls showed that Labour gained the majority of the working-class vote, though the Tories polled almost thirty per cent, mainly through deference. Mass Observation found that by far the main reason for voting Labour was class identity: 43 per cent gave this as their reason, compared to 6 per cent for nationalisation, the next specific reason. Labour seems to have made gains among both the more affluent workers, and among the poorer sections, such as farm labourers, the latter having previously often been non-voters. In class terms therefore, Labour's victory was basically a working-class one, a culmination of the growth of class consciousness, a class consciousness reflecting a variety of factors, including the growth of socialism, but more generally a negative rejection of, in Mass Observation's words, the ' "Them" who make vast profits', and belief that 'we' could have a better life.

A second common approach is to stress the views of the electorate. Many have seen the result in terms of the creation of, in Miliband's words, a new 'popular radicalism, more widespread than at any time in the previous hundred years'. Some have even argued that there was a revolutionary situation. Others, notably Paul Addison, have seen the electorate in more moderate terms, stressing the emergence of a reforming consensus.[21]

There is little evidence to support the existence of mass radicalism, let alone a revolutionary situation, though this is not to deny that some people and areas, such as the mining communities of South Wales, had strong left leanings. Polls showed considerable support for most of Labour's nationalisation proposals. However, some of Labour's plans were not strongly opposed by other parties. Polls further showed that nationalisation did not figure prominently in most electors' minds.

This should not be seen as supporting the existence of a reforming consensus. Mass Observation found that many people had few positive views. The Secretary of the Labour Party in his report on the election saw the result in part in negative terms, noting that 'There was a tidal wave of popular discontent which submerged the Tories.' People seem to have voted against the Tories as much as for Labour, to have rejected the values of a party identified with mass unemployment and poverty. To some extent there was a movement towards a more socialist ethic, a rejection of the ' "Them" who make vast profits' on moral grounds rather than envy. Nevertheless, overall this was hardly a reforming consensus; a rejecting consensus might be more apposite.

Some left-wing critics at the time, and since, have argued that the views of the electorate in part stemmed from Labour's own moderation. There is some force in this, though it is inconsistent with the more common left-wing argument that there was a radical electorate in 1945 (an inconsistency which has not stopped some critics, notably Coates, from using both arguments[22]). Subsequently, this was to provide another left-wing argument for more radical policies, but it was a difficult argument to prove, and moderates in the party after 1945 found it easier to point to the evidence of electoral moderation to support their own limited horizons. The evidence concerning the 1945 result therefore lent itself more readily to the moderates than the left, though the left in no way conceded its position.

However, these debates were to come later. In July 1945 Labour was euphoric rather than analytic. Labour was to form its first ever majority government.

Chapter Three

PREPARING TO GOVERN THE 'NEW' BRITAIN

i. Supplies and Services (Transitional Powers).
ii. Coal industry nationalisation.
iii. Nationalisation of the Bank of England.
iv. National Insurance (Industrial Injuries).
v. National Insurance.
vi. Town and country planning.
vii. Air transport.

Bills regarded of prime urgency by the Cabinet Committee on the King's Speech, 30 July 1945. Discussed in the Cabinet on 7 August. Cabinet Minutes (45) 18.

Part One: Cabinet Making and Government

For a short time on 26 July it was not clear whether Attlee would lead the first majority Labour administration. When it became certain that Labour would be forming a government, Attlee, Bevin, Morrison, and the party Secretary gathered in Bevin's room at Transport House. Morrison strongly argued that Attlee should not form a government before the PLP had met to elect its new officers. This proposal was in keeping with the spirit of the 1933 conference resolution on the formation of future Labour governments, though Morrison's suggestion was motivated by ambition rather than party niceties. Morrison had never completely accepted Attlee's victory over him in the 1935 leadership contest. He refused to accept that Attlee, a modest man with much to be modest about, a sheep in sheep's clothing, in Churchill's damning epithets, was more fitted to lead the party; he knew that even during the war there had been further moves to replace Attlee. During the meeting a phone call arrived from Cripps, who supported Morrison's demand for delay; Cripps had always thought that Attlee lacked charismatic appeal. However, Bevin's antipathy to 'that little bugger 'Erbert' had in no way diminished with the passing of the years; he had also grown to appreciate Attlee's qualities, especially as a manager of the coalition that made up the Labour Party. Bevin could well have challenged Attlee's leadership himself, but he had developed a great loyalty towards Attlee during the war years. One of his reasons for detesting Morrison was his belief that Morrison was an inveterate conspirator, that he was inherently disloyal. He therefore told Attlee not to wait.[1]

Attlee almost certainly needed no encouragement. Constitutional precedent favoured him. If the King offered him the commission, he could accept; if he failed, he could wait for the PLP to meet and elect a new leader. Similarly, the 1933 conference resolution did not specifically state that a leadership election should take place. Therefore, later on the evening of 26 July Attlee travelled to the Palace with Mrs Attlee in their little Standard 10 saloon. His mode of travel was in marked contrast to the chauffeur-driven limousine in which Churchill had been conveyed to tender his resignation. It remained to be seen if a Labour administration would offer as marked a change.

Having accepted the King's commission, Attlee set about constructing his government with speed. He ignored the 1933 conference resolution provision that he should appoint three 'advisers' to help him choose his Cabinet. As with the decision to form a government, he had no consultations with the NEC or other party organs, though he asked the permission of the PLP Administrative Committee to proceed to choose ministers, and some consultations with leading colleagues were undertaken.

Bevin was given the Foreign Office. He had wanted to be Chancellor of the Exchequer, but Attlee believed that there were likely to be troubles ahead with the Russians and considered Bevin, who had always held a strong hostility to both communism and the Soviet Union, would be more capable of handling these problems than Dalton. Giving Bevin the Foreign Office additionally kept him as far apart as possible from Morrison. Morrison was made Lord President of the Council, with special responsibility for coordinating the home front, Leader of the House of Commons, and deputy Prime Minister. Dalton was made Chancellor of the Exchequer. Cripps was made President of the Board of Trade. And Bevan was appointed Minister of Health, with particular responsibility for the important fields of housing and introducing a National Health Service; at forty-seven he was the youngest member of a somewhat aged Cabinet.[2]

The Cabinet contined twenty members, two fewer than were in the Cabinet immediately after the 1935 general election. It included representatives of the various ideologies and interests in the party. There were six union-sponsored MPs, proportionate to their number in the PLP as a whole.[3] On the other hand, the left was under-represented, with only Bevan in the Cabinet (Cripps's views had undergone a major change since the late 1930s). Class-wise, the government was also a co-alition. It included men of working-class origins, like Bevin and Bevan, though the life style of the latter was hardly working-class. It included middle-class members like Attlee, Cripps and Dalton. And it contained men like Morrison, products of that grey area where the middle class meets the working class.

In the 1930s Attlee had been a leading advocate of the small Cabinet, but this presented political problems in selection. The system of Cabinet committees used especially during the second world war similarly offered the advantages of specialisation, speed and coordination, while allowing a larger Cabinet overall. It was therefore decided from the outset to continue with this practice, though the wartime structure was reorganised to suit Labour's needs. A second major peacetime change was the use of coordinating ministers for various general fields of government, for example the Lord President's committee on economic policy.[4] Over this Cabinet structure presided Attlee with firm efficiency. For all the self-effacing, chairman-like style, Attlee took a major role in Cabinet from the outset, though he normally allowed ministers to get on with their jobs, and he certainly did not head a 'Prime Ministerial' government.[5] In particular, Attlee frequently consulted closely with some of his leading colleagues in what amounted to an inner Cabinet, including Bevin, sometimes Morrison, and later Cripps.

Within ministries there was some change of civil servants, but basically few alterations were made here. There had been some criticism in the party of the role of civil servants during the first two minority Labour governments, and there was ample evidence that ministers such as Snowden and Thomas were dominated by their civil servants. However, the failings of the 1924 and 1929-1931 governments tended, with good reason, to be put down to personality, or lack of policy rather than civil service sabotage. Scant attention was paid to the fact that the majority of top civil servants came from middle and upper class backgrounds, and that their views might not coincide with Labour's. During the war the service expanded rapidly, a development which prompted an inquiry by a 1943-1944 Departmental Committee. This made a series of comments about narrowness of outlook, the failure to use experts, and inefficiencies, but Labour made little attempt to act on any of these criticisms. In 1946 a Treasury Machinery of Government group began work, but this had been anticipated in a 1944 coalition report, and concerned itself mainly with the mechanics of government – though admittedly this was important in its own right. Also appointed in 1946 was a Cabinet committee on civil service manpower, but this again tended to ignore many central questions, though its work raised some important points. For example, a minute dated 10 April 1947 noted that an increase in the number of civil servants was expected, and that criticisms of civil servants as 'parasites on the community' would grow; it was argued that it would be necessary for the Prime Minister to 'underline the part which the Civil Service plays, and its contribution to the public good'.

Some have seen the civil service as a central problem in the enactment of Labour's programme; Marwick has even written that 'sometimes one has the impression that it was rather the Government which cooperated loyally with the civil servants'.[6] However, Labour could hardly have altered the nature of the whole service; many civil servants after 1945 were effectively neutral, even sympathetic; and examples of criticism or opposition to Labour's policies should not necessarily be seen as sabotage, especially as many of Labour's policies were vague. Nevertheless, Labour was undoubtedly wrong, both in terms of its beloved efficiency, and political control, not to pay more serious attention to the civil service in later years. The party's main defence is that it was already engaged in major administrative changes connected with its legislative programme. And in retrospect, the record of the government can better be understood in terms of the views of the Labour leaders and other factors, rather than civil service influence.

It is even more misleading to imply, as Miliband has done, that Labour policy was in any significant way influenced by the King.[7] Attlee was a great admirer of the King, and the King undoubtedly was willing to give advice on many issues. However, this does not mean that he was influential; the King advised Attlee to appoint Bevin Foreign Secretary, but later Attlee claimed that he did not remember this! If Labour policy at the time was conventional and moderate, it is important to remember that these words well describe its leadership too. Attlee was an intensely conventional man, a man who shuddered if the port was passed round the wrong way!; behind him stood a wife who was even suspected of Conservative tendencies!

Part Two: Programme, Parliament and Party

Parliament reassembled on 1 August. It was crowded to overflowing;

among Labour members there was a great sense of enthusiasm and expectation. Well over two hundred Labour members had not sat in Parliament before, a new generation of men, who included three future Labour leaders, Hugh Gaitskell, Harold Wilson, and James Callaghan. The Conservative members tried to put on a brave face, greeting Churchill with a hearty rendition of *For He's a Jolly Good Fellow*. Labour backbenchers replied with that apogee of collective Labour emotionalism, the *Red Flag*, though some of the new members clearly did not know the words. After the Speaker had been re-elected, with perhaps an even more suitable show of reluctance than usual, he felt it necessary to remark that he hoped he had been elected Speaker of the House of Commons, and not director of a musical chorus!

On 15 August, the day after Japan formally surrendered, Parliament gathered to hear the King's speech. This put forward a heavy programme for the first session, a programme which imposed a great strain on those who drafted the bills, the faceless but important legal brains who translate the government's will into the necessarily precise legal language. In spite of considerable wartime discussion in government departments of post-war reconstruction, draft legislation did not exist for many of the main planks of Labour's programme – particularly the nationalisation proposals, which in general had been considered too controversial by departments, a point ignored by many commentators.[8] The Parliamentary Counsel warned Morrison of the problems which Labour's programme posed. Morrison readily saw the difficulties and a Committee on the King's speech was established, chaired by Morrison, to consider which legislation should be taken first (after January 1946 the order of legislation was dealt with by the Future Legislation Committee). This committee did not include any departmental ministers, so there could be no question of ministerial interest. However, the choice of early legislation was to attract growing criticism in subsequent years.

Some of the measures clearly reflected a view of what was needed most urgently. It was believed that nationalisation of the Bank of England would provide fuller control; parts of the welfare legislation were thought to be desperately needed. On the other hand, some measures were not of great importance, for example the nationalisation of civil aviation. Some bills reflected pressures from interests within the party. The high priority for the nationalisation of the mines owed much to the fervent support of the NUM (as the MFGB became known in 1945), though it is true that the mines after the war needed government aid (but so did other industries). Similarly, the high priority given the new trade unions bill reflected union desires.

Both at the time, and later, much criticism was to focus on Labour not taking some of its more controversial legislation first, especially the nationalisation of iron and steel.[9] Nevertheless, it is not clear what advantages would have accrued from this. Labour was more united in 1945 than it was to be in 1948-1950, and business pressure groups were to become more active. But Labour was divided over iron and steel, and taking the measure earlier might have undermined some of the party's unity; it is also likely that the steel lobby would have put up strong opposition even in 1945-1946; besides, subsequent opposition did not prevent nationalisation. Furthermore, it is not clear that Labour could have introduced the bill in 1945-1946. The owners were not willing to cooperate, the bill was a complex one, which would take time to draft, and which would then be time-consuming in Parliament.

Many have linked calls for a more radical policy in the early years with a misreading of the mood of the country. Woodrow Wyatt, a moderate new Labour MP, reflected the opinion of many when he claimed that in the autumn of 1945 the country was well to the left of the government. Certainly in November 1945 Labour won sweeping victories in local elections, and in four out of the six by-elections in late 1945 there were further swings to Labour.[10] A Gallup poll after the 1945 election asked people whether they thought the result meant that the electorate wanted Labour to govern along existing lines, or to introduce sweeping changes, such as nationalisation. 56 per cent said the second, to 30 per cent for the first. However, these figures must be treated with caution. In particular, it is reasonable to ask how sweeping a change nationalisation represented in view of the way it was presented by Labour. Gallup and Mass Observation did not find any strong desire for specific radical legislation during 1945-1946. There was a radical potential, but it is doubtful whether iron and steel was the issue to arouse this potential.

It is important not to elevate the nationalisation of iron and steel into a socialist shibboleth; a case can be made that it was not especially significant. The steel industry was dominated by a small number of companies, and was generally in need of rationalisation, both factors which favoured Fabian efficiency arguments for nationalisation. Nevertheless, the commitment to iron and steel nationalisation owed more to TUC support, and pressure at the 1944 Labour conference for more nationalisation. As subsequent history was to prove, the control of iron and steel did not in any significant way further the cause of socialism, or give, as Addison has claimed, 'one of the most glittering prizes in the private sector', or in A.A. Rogow's words, 'crucial power over the economy' to the government.[11]

At a wider level, it is not clear what effect taking iron and steel early on would have had on international opinion, especially American. Immediately after 1931 there had been some discussion in the party about the international implications of a socialist government coming to power, and many feared that radical policies would lead to a financial crisis. The British economy was not isolated from the world, a point often played down by left-wing critics such as Miliband.[12] Britain would have had great difficulties surviving the immediate post-war problems without considerable aid. There is clear evidence that some in America were worried by Labour's early legislation, moderate as it was. By the time the iron and steel measure was introduced in 1948 America was firmly committed to aiding Britain, not least because of the beginning of the cold war.

The problems with Labour's legislation were not so much to do with priorities, as with the very nature of the programme itself — its intellectual flaws, reflection of piecemeal interests, and implicit assumption that legislation could fundamentally alter deeply held social beliefs. It is difficult to see how taking the 1945 programme in any other order would have produced a different Britain. Only another programme, and greater concentration on the ethical side of socialism, might have done this. And another, especially more radical, programme would have posed serious problems because of Britain's economic problems and need for aid.

In 1945 it was not clear to what extent an extensive reforming programme could be pushed quickly through Parliament. In the 1930s many on the left of the party had argued that Parliament could not cope with the legislative demands of a future socialist government; they had therefore advocated the use of an Emergency Powers Act and what amounted to rule by decree; they had also considered the abolition of the House of Lords a necessity. In 1945 Labour made no effort to make such radical changes. Even so, Labour did introduce some major changes in Parliamentary procedures in an effort to expedite the implementation of its programme.

At the first Cabinet meeting on 7 August Morrison stressed the need to use delegated legislation, and speed up the Parliamentary process. At the next meeting on 9 August the Chief Whip proposed that there should be no private members' time; this was agreed, and accepted by the Commons on 16 August. Later the Commons agreed to the abolition of taking the committee stage of all controversial bills on the floor of the whole House; this was reserved mainly for bills of constitutional importance. Subsequent changes included the removal of the limit on the number of standing committees, and a reduction in their maximum size. It was left to the government to decide how to make use of them, and during 1945-1950 the government made extensive use of committees.[13]

A variety of changes were made to facilitate government-backbench communication. The PLP elected a non-ministerial Chairman and Vice Chairman, but its regular Wednesday meetings were normally attended by ministers, especially Morrison. A Liaison Committee was established to which backbenchers could bring complaints, Morrison arranging for the relevant minister to be present. Morrison, as Leader of the House, also tried to keep an open-door policy. A further development was the establishment of committees of backbenchers to correspond with the major offices of the state, though this in some areas only formalised existing practice.

The size of Labour's majority meant that a relaxation of the strict Standing Orders on discipline could be allowed, and by 1946 a new set of rules had to be introduced. Subsequently, Labour discipline was to be less strong than in earlier Parliaments, and especially during 1929-1931. Dissent grew as the Parliament progressed, and five members of the PLP were to be expelled before 1950, but this was mainly for alleged communist sympathies and activities outside Parliament. The size of Labour's majority also allowed in 1946 the introduction of a three-group system which permitted one group to be absent from Parliament, while the other two retained a majority — an important asset in all-night sittings.[14]

In spite of these efforts to ease and clarify government-PLP relations, no attempt was made to resolve relations between the Parliamentary party and organisations in the country, especially conference. Since the 1907 conference gave the PLP the responsibility of deciding on the timing of the implementation of conference decisions, a right effectively confirmed in the 1918 constitution, there had been periodic friction over this issue. Attlee in the 1930s frequently referred to conference as the governing parliament of the movement. However, Attlee's disregard of the spirit of the 1933 conference resolution on the formation of future Labour governments showed either that his views had changed, or that his previous statement was misleading. The latter is nearer the truth. Conference retained an important role in Labour thinking, but none of the leaders wanted to have the hands of the government tied by conference resolutions, or by the NEC. This in part reflected a certain élitism, but it also reflected fears about the representativeness of constituency and especially union delegations. The Labour Party was certainly no internal democracy, as writers like Samuel Beer have tended to imply, but nor was its power structure the essentially oligarchical one depicted by Robert McKenzie.[15]

Individual membership of the Labour Party in 1945 amounted to 487,047, but only a fraction of this number were genuinely active. In many constituency parties a handful of people dominated policy making, and there were no definite controls over conference mandating. Furthermore, since the late 1930s there had been some efforts by communists, and to a lesser extent Trotskyites, to operate under cover in the constituencies. Naturally, these factors tended to make the leadership cautious about policy demands and statements from local parties.

There were 2,510,369 affiliated union members in 1945. The power wielded by the unions at conference through their block votes had been a frequent source of criticism in the past, especially in the 1930s. Even after a reform at the 1937 conference which increased the constituency parties' representation on the NEC, and allowed them to elect their own representatives, the unions retained the vast majority of NEC seats, and votes at conference. This situation not only provoked constituency party criticism, but also made the leadership wary of considering conference truly democratic, particularly as communists were highly active in some unions.

Nevertheless, it is important not to think that there was a clear constituency party-trade union split, or that the union block votes were always cast in the same way. Moreover, by 1945 much of the friction in this sphere had disappeared. The union leadership was also less assertive than it had been after 1931. The party was relatively united over a programme which included many union desires; the most dominant union leader was at the Foreign Office, and wielded considerable influence in the party's inner circles. Behind the scenes there were still some problems; for example, Citrine protested about the lack of references to trade unions in an early draft of the Labour manifesto, and the TUC General Council clearly expected to be consulted closely by the government.[16] But in public all was peace in the Labour movement, a remarkable change from the late 1930s. It was a situation which augured well for the new government.

Chapter Four

'WE ARE THE MASTERS NOW', 1945-1946

'We are the masters at the moment, and not only at the moment, but for a very long time to come.'

Sir Hartley Shawcross, the Attorney-General winding up the Third Reading of the Trade Disputes and Trade Unions Bill, 2 April 1946. *House of Commons Parliamentary Debates*, Volume 421, number 113, column 1217. This became popularly abbreviated to 'We are the masters now.'

Part One: Legislation and Reform

Labour in the late summer of 1945 was ecstatic, the mass of its members exhilarated at the prospect of majority office, its leaders feeling that they were walking with destiny as they began to implement the policies which they believed would create the new socialist Britain.[1] The Conservatives, particularly in Parliament, were in a state of shock; the *Tribune* on 30 November cheekily enquired 'What, no opposition?'

The nationalisation programme was prepared and coordinated by two main committees: an Official Committee on the Socialisation of Industries, chaired by a senior Treasury official and dealing with the more administrative aspects, and a Ministerial Committee, chaired by Morrison and dealing with more general questions. Morrison, who had been the minister responsible for working out the details for the establishment of the London Passenger Transport Board during 1929-1931, took an especially strong interest in the nationalisation programme, and the relevant ministers frequently consulted him over their plans. Morrison's guiding role, and the coordinating activities of the various committees, helped ensure that there were strong similarities in Labour's nationalisation measures.[2]

The first nationalisation measure passed was the Bank of England Act. Some at the time, and others since, have argued that this measure was unnecessary.[3] It is true that the government already exercised a large degree of control, but there were times when the Bank seemed more a law unto itself, not least during the 1929-1931 Labour government. The act additionally gave the Bank of England the right to issue directives to the joint stock banks, a provision opposed by the Governor of the Bank, but he was overruled on this, and other issues. Dalton, the minister specifically responsible for the bill, was later to write that power had been transferred from the City to the Chancellor of the Exchequer. This view was even more mistaken than the judgement that nationalisation had changed nothing.

In the early 1930s the left had argued for the nationalisation of the whole banking system, a policy narrowly carried at the 1932 conference. However, this owed more to the currency of the 'bankers' ramp' theory of Labour's fall in 1931 than to any theoretical appreciation of the role of banking. Nationalisation was opposed by strong forces in the party. Bevin and many of the union leadership were unconvinced of the necessity of the measure; banking was not a field which attracted any great amount of trade union interest, and as late as 1944 the TUC policy statement on post-war reconstruction did not give a high priority even to the national-isation of the Bank of England. Morrison and others thought that national-isation of the joint stock banks would be electorally disastrous, remember-ing the Post Office savings scare in the 1931 general election. Dalton, and later the rising young Labour intellectuals Evan Durbin and Hugh Gaitskell, challenged the need to nationalise the banks on economic grounds. They argued that banks were not the major source of industrial finance, a point borne out by the experience of the 1945-1951 government, though this period also saw the banks to some extent resisting government policy as regards the direction of investment.[4] They believed that the control of the Bank of England would be sufficient to ensure prosperity, a belief encouraged in the late 1930s by growing interest in Keynesian macro-economic policy. Therefore in 1945 Labour made no effort to control the banking and insurance system as a whole.

Furthermore, the manner of nationalisation did not involve a radical change. There was no attempt to change the Governor, or Deputy Governor; the board, or Court, was left virtually the same. Nationalisation was accompanied by full compensation. Nevertheless, this policy had some justifications. In particular, there was a feeling that a massive change of personnel might have undermined confidence in the banking and industrial system, which remained basically capitalist. The impact of changes at the Bank, and more generally of paying less than full compensation, must additionally be seen against a background of the attitudes of foreign bankers, and British business confidence.

The second nationalisation measure was coal.[5] If nationalisation of the Bank of England reflected the priority of Labour's moderate intellectuals, coal represented the fervent desires of the unions, notably the miners, who in 1945 accounted for 423,085 of Labour's 2,510,369 affiliated unionists, and were strongly represented in the government. Every faceworker carried blue scars on his body, old wounds filled with coal dust; disabled men filled the streets, and corpses the cemetries – the human price of coal. For many miners nationalisation had nothing to do with efficency and rationalisation; it was to bring salvation.

Churchill, speaking in Parliament in August, accepted nationalisation, as he had done with the Bank of England, though this did not stop the Conservatives voting against the second reading of both bills. The coal owners' federation in September also agreed to cooperate. However, it is important not to conclude that the Conservatives would necessarily have introduced similar legislation. Many have claimed that all Labour's nationalisation was accepted by earlier Conservative-dominated committees of inquiry.[6] But the Reid Committee on the mines in 1945 did not support public ownership; indeed, none of the relevant committees, with the exception of the Heyworth Committee on gas, which reported after the general election, recommended nationalisation. Following on the Reid Committee, the mine owners in 1945 produced a report accepting government aid, though rejecting nationalisation; this was Conservative policy as well. The point is that after Labour came to office the owners and Conservatives did not feel strongly enough to oppose the measure vigorously, especially after so decisive a Labour victory.

In spite of the nationalisation of coal being one of Labour's oldest demands, the Minister of Fuel and Power, Emmanuel Shinwell, found that Labour did not possess a fully worked out nationalisation scheme. The Committee on the King's Speech had placed coal nationalisation before the Bank of England, but the introduction of the measure was delayed because it proved a more complicated bill to draw up. The Bank of England involved one clearly defined organisation; there were eight hundred different coal companies, and increasing company integration meant that coal companies operated in other fields – where should the line be drawn for nationalisation? There were other problems over the structure of the industry, compensation, and so on. Indeed, the bill introduced in the House of Commons on 19 December 1945 was the twelfth printed draft!

The structure of control and management proposed for coal was basically to be followed in subsequent nationalisation measures. The industry was organised on a national level. During the inter-war years Labour thought had become increasingly concerned with strong central-isation as a means of ensuring power and uniformity. However, this development also raised major problems in running large scale industry and also in terms of industrial democracy. At the top was a public board. Many in the unions preferred this to ministerial control, mainly because it offered the opportunity for union nomination to the board, a policy which had been accepted at the 1933 Labour conference, though the 1944 TUC post-war policy statement had argued that direct representation would undermine the unions' independence. For those of Fabian persua-sion the board offered the opportunity of the technocrats ruling for greater efficiency. Some pointed to the increasing divorce of ownership and control, and claimed that a managerial group was already emerging which was not obsessed by corporate and personal profit. In retrospect, this argument was overstated, but critics such as Marwick have failed to take into account its appeal at the time.[7]

In his second reading speech Shinwell stated that the members of the board would be chosen 'because they possess the appropriate qualifica-tions for running an industry of such complexity and magnitude'. The board consisted of nine members. The Chairman was Lord Hyndley, who had been managing director of the Powell-Duffryn coal mining giant, an appointment which has been strongly criticised by writers such as Coates.[8] However, Hyndley had long favoured nationalisation and was well liked by many of the miners' leaders. Of the other eight members of the first board, only two were unionists – the secretaries of the TUC and NUM, who resigned their posts so that they would not be direct representatives. The presence of only two union members on the board has also been criticised, but in part this stemmed from an unwillingness on the part of the unions to release leading officials for service on boards.

At the lower levels of industry no attempt was made to introduce any form of workers' control, again a pattern to be followed in later nationalisation. The union leaders in general had little time for any mean-ingful form of workers' control; the unions were often bureaucratically organised, and workers' control had implications for intra-union as well as industrial power. Furthermore, as in the case of the boards, there was a belief that independence would increase rather than decrease power.[9] The miners, internally one of the most democratic unions, had proposed a system of worker representation to the 1919 Sankey Commission on the coal industry, but as syndicalist and guild socialist ideas faded from view in the 1920s, so did the miners' strong commitment to workers' control decline. This decline in part reflected the growing strength of the Fabian tradition, its emphasis on Parliament as the true expression of majority will, and faith in the expert. Cripps illustrates this point well. In a speech in Bristol on 27 October 1946 this former leader of the Labour left exhibited a classic Fabian efficiency-managerialism when he argued that the working class as a whole did not contain enough people with administrative skills to be allowed any form of industrial control.

Miliband and others have since quoted this against Cripps, and generally criticised the Labour governments for failing to change the power structure within nationalised industries.[10] These criticisms raise important points, but it is vital to remember that the absence of any provision for workers' control stemmed from far more than business opposition; there was powerful opposition in the party, though there was also considerable support among the rank and file. Moreover, major questions about the nature of workers' control, and its place in a mixed market economy, linked to a world economy, remained unresolved.

The question of compensation for nationalisation was another controversial one. Compensation divided the early Labour Party, but by the 1930s most of the leadership had come to accept a policy of nationalisation on full compensation. Although this was bitterly criticised by many on the left, such as Cripps, party policy held that compensation would smooth the transition period to nationalisation, and generally promote confidence.

The 'net maintainable revenue' formula, used by Morrison for the London Passenger Transport Board, was chosen for coal. Compensation was paid in government stock, and set at £164,660,000, against a mine owners' valuation of £233,500,000. Although the bill received the Royal Assent in August 1946, it was to be 1949 before all claims were settled, an indication of the problems that can result from compensation. Compensation further meant that the mine owners' wealth was preserved. However, any attempt to nationalise without compensation, or on low compensation, would have caused problems in the transition period when private owners remained in charge of the mines. Such a policy would also have had serious effects on other industries likely to be nationalised, the whole business community, and on international confidence, points usually ignored by Miliband and other left-wing critics.[11]

A final point concerns pricing policy. Shinwell during the second reading specifically stated that the National Coal Board would not seek to put prices at a level designed to bring in the maximum profit; the NCB by statute was only expected to cover costs. Even this proved difficult in an overmanned and often backward industry. Some ministers, notably Bevan, argued that it was not necessary for a nationalised industry to cover costs, or make a profit; that social, or other reasons might justify a deficit. This was not popular with most ministers. Nevertheless, price rises were usually less than those asked for by the NCB to cover costs. Coal was therefore sold with a hidden subsidy to consumers and business; at the same time the NCB's non-profitability proved a godsend to anti-nationalisation propagandists who could easily equate efficiency with profit (or in the NCB's case, the lack of profit).

Two further pieces of nationalisation completed the programme for the first session. The first was civil aviation. During the war the coalition had produced a plan for post-war reorganisation, which envisaged substantial state control, but left some role for private enterprise. In October 1945 the Labour Cabinet agreed that the whole industry should be nationalised, though allowing private operators in the charter field. This was embodied in the 1946 Civil Aviation Act. The last piece of nationalisation in this session was the taking over of Cable and Wireless. Cable and Wireless· Limited operated a telecommunications network between Britain and many of the Commonwealth countries. At a meeting of Commonwealth governments in 1944 it had been agreed to set up a public utility corporation in each country. Although Cable and Wireless objected, in February 1946 the Legislation Committee decided that a bill could be fitted into the session, and the bill passed into law later in 1946.[12]

High priority was given to the Trade Disputes and Trade Unions Bill. In 1927, following the general strike, the Conservative government had introduced a new trade union act. In brief, this outlawed the sympathetic and general strike, made picketing fraught with legal dangers, forced union members to contract into, rather than out of, the political levy, banned civil service unions from affiliating to the TUC, and made compulsory membership of a union in local government illegal, at the same time making it more difficult to strike. This act was generally hated throughout the Labour movement, and the 1946 act basically restored the *status quo ante*. There were some criticisms that this left many ambiguities in the law, but it had the immediate effect in the TUC of allowing the affiliation of nearly 350,000 civil servants; it further substantially increased the Labour Party's income through the political levy (the percentage paying the levy rose from 48.5 per cent in 1945 to 90.6 per cent in 1947). Conservative MPs vigorously attacked the provisions of the act, and its high priority at a time of economic crisis. Labour members again sang the *Red Flag* in the division lobbies; to the trade unionists the act meant a great deal.[13]

The trade unions were far less directly concerned with Labour's social welfare legislation. This was dealt with by two main ministries, National Insurance and Health. A Social Services Cabinet committee was appointed, chaired by Arthur Greenwood, the Lord Privy Seal. Greenwood was a popular figure in the party; he had been elected Treasurer at the 1943 conference, defeating Morrison. In 1941 he had been appointed Minister without Portfolio in the Churchill coalition, charged with the task of studying post-war reconstruction, but had quickly shown that efficient administration was beyond him. The main onus of preparing legislation therefore fell on the departmental ministers — James Griffiths at National Insurance, and Bevan at Health.[14]

The main task of the Ministry of National Insurance was to implement parts of the Beveridge Report, and the 1944 White Paper on social insurance which was based on it. These promised an all-embracing social insurance scheme from the 'cradle to the grave', a system which would give people benefits as of right, and without a means test. However, although in some ways the Beveridge Report was a milestone in British social policy, in other ways it was not that radical, reflecting its author's essentially moderate philosophy — his interest in social administration rather than social welfare, in institutions rather than people.[15]

The social insurance part of the Beveridge Report had three major sets of flaws. First, Beveridge believed that benefits should be paid only at subsistence level, for to pay more would encourage idleness. Beveridge believed that subsistence could be calculated 'scientifically'. He failed to take notice of the fact that some wants are socially determined, that the poorest especially do not buy the unappetising foods recommended by medical experts, no matter how nutritious.[16] Secondly, the scheme continued the Lloyd George system in that it was an insurance scheme, a regressive form of taxation, that furthermore tied benefits to contributions. The insurance aspect additionally meant that some would not qualify for benefits. Beveridge proposed to cover this gap with a National Assistance scheme, but here benefits would be means-tested. Finally, benefits did not cover those in employment, even if 'scientifically' they were in need of assistance.

Labour in its 1946 National Insurance Act followed the outlines of these proposals (though the establishment of National Assistance was deferred until 1948). Labour had little other choice. The Beveridge Report had aroused great public support. Besides, Labour had nothing to put in its place. Social policy was an area which had not attracted great interest among the activists and intellectuals before the war. Some in the trade unions were even hostile to many aspects of welfare policy, believing that benefits undermined bargaining power, or holding self-help views.[17]

Labour made some detailed changes to the wartime proposals, alterations which have been frequently criticised: many have even claimed that Labour's system was inferior to Beveridge's.[18] In reality, these changes sometimes followed the spirit of Beveridge, sometimes they were less generous, and in one case they were more generous. The rates of benefit were calculated by adding 31 per cent to the figures which Beveridge worked out at 1938 prices. In 1945 prices stood at forty-eight per cent above the 1938 level, but Griffiths's proposals were consistent with Beveridge's subsistence views, for his figure of 31 per cent was based on the old 'working-class' cost of living index, which formed the basis of Dalton's promise in 1945 to hold the cost of living at 31 per cent above the pre-war level. Another change concerned unemployment benefit. Dalton strongly attacked continual payments at the 6 December Cabinet, pointing out that the cost of the whole scheme being proposed was £562 million in 1948, compared to £486 million proposed in the coalition White Paper. The Cabinet therefore agreed to limit payment to thirty weeks, partly because it was felt that there would be full employment, and that the long-term unemployed would include many 'work-shy' people. Dalton objected even more strongly to the cost of the old age pension provisions, which the government actuary expected to account for half the total expenditure on national insurance. Beveridge had proposed that the pensions scheme would be phased in over twenty years, but Griffiths planned to introduce his scheme immediately, a decision which the Cabinet accepted.

Griffiths additionally introduced a National Insurance (Industrial Injuries) Bill. Accidents at work were made a responsibility of society, and all workers were insured against such accidents. Labour again basically inherited the bill from the coalition, though on 9 October the Cabinet decided to increase the scale of benefits, and to make other changes, as a result of pressures from the TUC and NUM. These rates were therefore at a higher level than those for other benefits (this had been recommended by Beveridge).

Not everyone entitled to benefits claimed, and the rates were hardly excessive. Nevertheless, the new system was considered a notable advance in the field of social security, especially in its universality. Many subsequent critics who have pointed to the fact that the changes were only mildly redistributive have failed to appreciate how the change was seen at the time. Richard Titmuss was later to write, 'Many of us must now . . . admit that we put too much faith in the 1940s in the concept of universality as applied to social security. Mistakenly, it was linked with economic egalitarianism.'[19]

The Ministry of Health was mainly concerned with introducing a National Health Service, and with housing.

Before the second world war the provision of free health services had been very limited. The Lloyd George scheme left most people uncovered. Many people had to rely on private insurance, or on charity, on the voluntary hospitals which had regular flag days to raise money, which even sold advertising space on their walls to patent medicine manufacturers. Some doctors were forced to practise Robin Hood medicine, where they charged the rich heavily, so that they could help the poor; but not all doctors operated such policies. Certainly doctors in general gathered in the wealthier areas where they could hope to earn more; they followed the doctor in A.J. Cronin's 1930s classic novel, *The Citadel*, from the valleys to the metropolis.

In the early 1930s the Socialist Medical Association, which was affiliated to the Labour Party, pressed for a 'Socialised Medical Service', but the 1937 *Immediate Programme* limited itself to the vague promise that the 'Health Services will be extended'. It was the outbreak of war which prompted serious attention being paid to the health services. During the war the state took an increasing role in the provision and direction of medical services. The Beveridge Report, following on from the Medical Planning Commission, recommended a national health service, and a 1944 White Paper set out some of the details of such a scheme.[20]

The 1944 White Paper proposed a universal free system, financed by the Exchequer, local rates and an insurance element. Central responsibility for the service was given to the Minister of Health. Hospitals would be grouped under local authorities, themselves rationalised into larger units for this purpose. These authorities would be encouraged to set up health centres for doctors to work in. Doctors in the centres would be paid a salary, those outside would receive a capitation fee for all patients within the system registered with them. The sale of practices by GPs was to be banned, though the White Paper seemed to accept that private practice would continue. On other issues, such as the role of specialists in the system, it was even more vague.

These proposals ran into serious opposition from the main doctors' pressure group, the British Medical Association.[21] Its leadership, notably

Dr Guy Dain and Dr Charles Hill, strongly opposed any form of state control. A 'Questionary' of its membership revealed that the majority opposed the White Paper, though there was considerable support for the idea of a free system. There was a strong fear of organisation, and a professional fear of control; a salaried service was especially disliked, and the ending of the selling of practices was opposed by some, though the White Paper promised compensation. The doctors further disliked the prospect of municipal control. Municipal hospitals tended to be bad, and local government was the home of the lower middle-class, even working-class official. Faced with this criticism, the Conservative Minister of Health, Henry Willink, decided to enter into what amounted to negotiations, and began to back down on some of the White Paper's suggestions.

The new minister was Bevan, long an advocate of a free national system.[22] Bevan believed he could get what he wanted from the BMA, and he stopped the negotiations which had been taking place. However, this did not stop him addressing medical audiences (at one such meeting he claimed that he was a comparative virgin in medical affairs; Dain tartly replied that no such condition was known to medical science). More importantly, Bevan continued to take advice and 'consult' medical opinion, particularly the leaders of the Royal Colleges of Medicine. Lord Moran, the head of the Royal College of Physicians, became a frequent 'consultant' to Bevan. Almost certainly these contacts played a major role in convincing Bevan that he should make concessions to the specialists in his bill, which was published in March 1946.

The bill in many ways followed the lines of the 1944 White Paper, but with some important changes. In particular, all hospitals were to be taken over by the state (with the exception of the teaching hospitals). They were to be run regionally by fourteen boards, appointed by the minister, and through local management committees. Within the hospitals, the consultants were allowed to retain some private beds, as well as receiving a salary for cooperating with the state scheme. Local authorities retained some functions: they were to promote health centres, and were given responsibilities in fields like clinics, and the ambulance service. The 1946 bill also included from the outset dental, opthalmic and hearing services, which the 1944 proposals had intended only slowly to integrate.

This bill had already aroused some criticism. In particular, on 18 October in Cabinet Morrison opposed the reduction in power of the local authorities, especially in view of the fact that they were in part being replaced by 'non-democratic' regional boards; Morrison even claimed that local government 'might be dangerously undermined'. After the bill was published, it aroused further criticism in the party as a whole. There were objections to the failure to introduce a full salaried system, particularly as private practice was to be allowed to continue and private beds allowed in the hospitals. The Heads of the Royal Colleges had told Bevan that the beds were necessary to stop consultants setting up nursing homes, and Bevan accepted their demands as he was keen to have the best in the NHS. However, private practice certainly encouraged a two-standard system. Bevan told the Cabinet on 8 January 1946 that a two-tier system could be avoided by ensuring a high standard in the NHS, but he had little conception of the costs involved in a high-standard universal scheme. Moreover, it is not clear that the concession was necessary. There was massive public support for the NHS. High salaries might have been used to tempt the consultants in, together with promises of well-provided hospitals; although this would have raised other problems, they would have been preferable to allowing the continuation of a two-standard system.

Criticism over these questions was silenced somewhat in the Labour Party as a result of the bitter hostility with which the bill was greeted by the BMA. Added to its earlier arguments, was a strong attack on the nationalisation of the hospitals. Conservative criticism further silenced Labour opposition to the bill. The Conservatives' protestations of support for a NHS during the war should not be seen as implying that they would have introduced a measure anything like Labour's; Willink's negotiations and concessions clearly show that Conservative opposition in the House of Commons during 1946 was not simply party tactics. This can also be seen in the hostile attitude taken to the bill by sections of the press which supported the Conservative Party.

Nevertheless, the BMA and Conservatives failed to obtain any significant concessions, and the bill received the Royal Assent in November 1946. However, the fight was not over, and the BMA was to conduct a long rearguard action before the act came into force in July 1948.

Bevan was also in charge of the housing programme. *Let Us Face the Future* had stated that there should be a ministry combining Health's housing powers with the Ministry of Town and Country Planning's planning powers. This did not take place, and housing responsibilities fell rather uneasily between these ministries, and the Ministry of Works. Bevan's exertions in the NHS further meant that his attention could not be devoted fully to housing's needs, though part of the trouble was a lack of appreciation of the immense difficulties.

Housing had been the issue which concerned voters most during the

1945 election. There had been serious housing problems in many areas before the war. During the war nearly one in three houses had been damaged, and many more gone without repair. Overall, there were 700,000 fewer homes than in 1939.[23] Some preparations had been taken under the coalition, but coalition planning, and especially Conservative thinking, believed that the main task of house building in the post-war period would be undertaken by private enterprise, without strong government controls. Before the war private enterprise had been successful in building many houses — 355,000-374,000 a year in the late 1930s. However, this was achieved only after a slump which lowered costs and provided plentiful labour. Houses were also built mainly for sale to the middle class, though these houses were often of low standard. In the inter-war years only one in fifteen houses was built to clear Britain's extensive slums, a damning indictment of the 'social efficiency' of the free market.

Bevan decided to make radical changes.[24] On 9 October he told the Cabinet that the building industry needed to be controlled strictly. A system of licensing was introduced to control repairs and non-essential building. Local authorities were to be encouraged to plan a building programme. Bevan sought to reverse the pre-war rate of building three houses for private purchase to one for council use, to five to one in the opposite direction. Subsidies from the Exchequer were increased. Bevan also tried to promote variety, quality, and less realistically, a social 'mix' in housing. A New Towns Bill was introduced by the Minister of Town and Country Planning, following on the work of Lord Reith's wartime New Towns Committee. This further sought to place house-building powers in public hands. The large cities had grown too large, and there was a social need to move people away from these conurbations. The act provided for the setting up of Development Corporations, financed by the Exchequer, to promote new towns in desirable areas.

By May 1946 the building workforce was restored to its pre-war level, but only 55,811 new houses were built. Although a considerable number were repaired, and house building had to compete for resources with industry, this was not an impressive total. The attempts to license non-essential repairs ran into serious difficulties; there was a shortage of materials. Some local authorities, especially the smaller ones, were not enthusiastic about their new role. Bevan had not adequately considered whether they could undertake his programme, although this has not stopped some critics considering his efforts to have been an important contribution to housing policy.[25] Nevertheless, by late 1946 the housing problem seemed as bad as ever, and a sudden increase in the birth rate at the end of the war was threatening to make things worse. Squatting began on a major scale.

The Conservatives launched a series of telling attacks on Labour's housing record; they alleged that socialism meant inefficiency. These attacks augured badly for Labour. They were on an issue which greatly troubled the electorate. It was also easier for the Conservatives to cry inefficiency, than for Labour to point out the implicit values in this concept, and the social justice of its effort. However, during 1945-1946 these attacks did not detract from the general Labour euphoria. Labour maintained a firm lead in opinion polls, and seemed to be implementing a major legislative programme.

Other reforms introduced during this hectic first session included a Rent Act, strengthening control over furnished tenancies, the introduction of free school milk, orange juice and cod liver oil, and more expenditure on the universities, art galleries and on state forests. Many of these changes were introduced relatively quietly in budgets, and emphasise that it is important not simply to consider the major Labour measures. Dalton was especially proud of increasing investment in the forests, a reflection of an environmental more than economic concern.

Part Two: Economic Policy

Labour's changes in Cabinet structure in 1945 were designed in part to help coordinate economic policy. Labour's policy involved a significant increase in government intervention in the economy during peacetime, though there had been a high degree of control during the second world war.[26] *Let Us Face the Future* promised to plan 'from the ground up', and to maintain full employment. Economic policy therefore needed careful coordination.[27]

Morrison headed a group of ministers responsible for economic development and planning. His Lord President's Committee was the main committee dealing with economic affairs, though there was also a Ministerial Economic Planning Committee. Morrison was responsible for general coordination and physical controls over the economy. Dalton ran budgetary policy at the Treasury, and Cripps at the Board of Trade dealt with industry. There was additionally a series of inter-departmental civil service committees dealing with economic policy, and Economic Section of the Cabinet Office, and a small section of the Lord President's Office dealing with economic questions. George Isaacs at the Ministry of Labour often joined the highest-level discussions because of problems associated with demobilisation, and later labour shortages.

Many physical controls were taken over from the wartime coalition. A Supplies and Services (Transitional Powers) Act continuing wartime regulation of certain commercial, financial and industrial activities was one of the first measures passed by the government. The use of controls had long been part of Labour's plans, but it was generally agreed between the parties that some controls would be necessary after 1945, even if there was less agreement about their extent, duration and ultimate purpose. It was felt that without controls there might be economic chaos during the transition to peacetime; many remembered the troubles after the first world war when controls had been ended rapidly!

Labour's controls tended to be piecemeal, mainly seeking to restrict domestic demand and inflationary pressures, to prevent the production of 'non-essential' goods, and encourage exports. The bulk buying of food by the government, and general import controls continued; so did exchange controls; but some other controls were relaxed. A Capital Issues Committee continued the wartime practice of vetting new issues on to the capital market, a policy which had some success in directing investment into priority areas, though only issues over £50,000 were controlled.[28] In 1946 a National Investment Council was established, but this was designed to do little more than stimulate investment to promote full employment, mainly in the depressed areas; there was no serious attempt to interfere with private industry and control the direction of all investment. Similarly, manpower planning involved little more than ordered demobilisation with a sense of industrial priorities, as well as fairness to long-serving conscripts. Subsequently the government was to argue that the direction of manpower was one of the controls that differentiated a totalitarian system from democratic planning.

There were some moves during 1945-1946 towards more long-term macro-economic planning, a trend which would probably not have occurred under a Conservative government. The Official Steering Committee on Economic Policy as early as September 1945 decided to draw up a national plan. However, nothing along these lines appeared publicly before 1947, though an embryonic Economic Survey was discussed by the Cabinet as early as 7 February 1946. Many, especially on the left of the party, called for a more urgent approach to macro-economic planning, but these criticisms ignored the fact that such work takes time to prepare, though it is true that the government did not devote many resources to gathering relevant information. In this sphere again Labour came to office with no detailed plans or information, and foreign trade, one of the central

problems, was an issue almost totally ignored in earlier Labour discussion
of planning.

Labour tried to help the implementation and formulation of its planning by maintaining friendly relations with industry, and its representative
organisations, such as the Federation of British Industry. Many ministries
contained industrialists 'imported' to help with physical controls during
the war, for example the Board of Trade and Ministry of Food. Government bodies, such as the Cotton and Timber Controls, which bought raw
materials, were staffed largely by industrialists, again continuing wartime
practice. The government encouraged trade associations to speak for
whole industries. Labour retained certain bodies set up to increase consultation during the war. The National Production Advisory Council of
Industry, including representatives from industry, the TUC and civil
service, met at bi-monthly intervals to consider questions concerning
industry and production. A similar National Joint Advisory Council
considered labour questions.

Labour's sponsorship of these bodies, and later similar organisations
concerning planning and dollar exports, raises questions about corporatist tendencies in the party and Britain — the growth of contacts and
institutional linkages between government, business and unions.[29] In
part this stemmed from economic changes, such as increasing cartelisa-
tion and coordination within industries, but such concentration and
cooperation cohered well with Fabianism and the views of some union
leaders. Fabianism's emphasis on efficiency, the neutral expert, and
institutional formats encouraged a belief in the possibilities of such cooperation; and the unions since the late 1920s had been pursuing a policy
of industrial conciliation, and seeking various forms of greater consultation. Nevertheless, it is important not to overstate corporatist tendencies
at this time, or see them in developments which have other explanations.

Miliband has claimed that private industry cooperated with the government, 'Or, more accurately, private industry enjoyed the cooperation of
the Government.'[30] However, this implicit division of interest is in some
ways misleading. The interests of private industry and government were
not necessarily the same, but nor were they necessarily different, especially
during the transition to peacetime. Moreover, it has to be remembered
that one reason why the government relied so heavily on businessmen
was the shortage of suitable civil servants to take planning posts. Here
was a major reason why Labour should have paid more careful attention
to the civil service, though part of this neglect stemmed from a growing
tendency to see planning as only a short-term policy.

After 1945 there was mounting interest in the use of budgetary policy to secure economic goals, notably full employment, which had been accepted as an economic aim in the 1944 White Paper on *Employment Policy*. Since Keynes's arrival at the Treasury in the early part of the war, there had been a commitment to the use of the budget to regulate aggregate demand, though in the war physical controls were far more important.

In his first two budgets in October 1945 and April 1946 Dalton reduced income tax from 10 to 9 shillings in the pound, thus reversing the old Labour support for high income taxes and low indirect taxes, which were seen as regressive, though surtax and death duties were raised. Taxes during the war had been increased to high levels, and although at the end of the war there were fears about a sudden increase in demand, and desire to promote exports, it was felt that cuts were necessary as incentives. Dalton was also especially keen to keep prices of basic goods steady, and promised that if necessary subsidies, introduced in 1941, would be increased to achieve this. He further cut, and then repealed, the wartime Excess Profits Tax as part of a policy to stimulate investment.

A cheap money policy was another major aspect of Dalton's policy, though this again continued wartime practice, and was supported by the Bank of England and Treasury. Dalton was keen to keep long-term interest rates down to 2-3 per cent for a variety of reasons. He claimed that it would mean cheap nationalisation, for it reduced the cost of government borrowing. Similarly, it would help the local authorities borrow for the housing programme. Dalton further believed that low rates would mean 'euthanasia for the *rentier*'. Cheap money was additionally seen as an encouragement to general investment; it is important to remember that the bogy of stagnation was still very much in some experts' minds.[31]

Dalton was subsequently to claim that full employment was 'the greatest revolution brought about by the Labour government'.[32] Certainly employment figures in post-war Britain differed drastically from the pre-war situation. In 1938 unemployment had averaged 1,859,000, or 13.5 per cent, and at its peak in 1933 it has been almost 3,000,000. In 1946 unemployment was 431,000, or 2.5 per cent. However, it is far from clear that these changes stemmed from Labour's economic policy. A strong case can be made that full employment stemmed from an increase in investment, itself mainly a result of a cyclical boom engendered by the war, though the coalition and Labour's commitment to full employment and other policies on investment may have conditioned entrepreneurial expectations to some extent.[33] Dalton's cheap money policy may also have been inflationary. His Parliamentary Private Secretary,

Evan Durbin, who was a professional economist, certainly argued this. The price index was undoubtedly rising. The working-class index rose from 156 in 1938 to 203 in 1945, where it was stabilised until 1947; prices in general were rising, and the new index introduced in 1947 provides a better picture, standing at 108 by 1948. Nevertheless, it would be wrong to attribute this increase simply to the cheap money policy.

Labour's economic policy has to be seen against a background of serious economic difficulties, in particular over the balance of payments. War had been disastrous for Britain. The sale of foreign assets to pay for the war amounted to £1,118 million, leaving net investment income from abroad at half the 1938 level; the rise in the price of imports meant that the net spending power of this income was one fifth. Commonwealth and other countries had run up sterling balances in London on a massive scale, Britain's indebtedness to these countries rising from £476 to £3,555 million during the war. This threatened a serious future instability should there be anything other than the strictest exchange controls. War had led to internal disinvestment through failure to replace plant and machinery to the extent of £2,500 million. Demobilisation would clearly cause transitional problems, as would returning factories to peacetime conditions. These, and many other, problems faced Labour on taking office.

The coalition's planning for the transition to peacetime assumed that these problems would be eased by continuing American aid, especially as the war against Japan was expected to last eighteen months after the end of the European war. It therefore came as a shock when on 21 August, six days after the Japanese surrender, the Americans announced the immediate end to Lend-Lease aid. (This was strictly in accordance with the original agreement, but many in the British government suspected that President Truman, who had taken office only shortly before, had been rushed into the decision by advisers who were unsympathetic to a Labour-governed Britain, or indeed any foreign commitments.)

Already on 14 August Dalton had circulated to the Cabinet a Keynes memorandum which pointed to Britain's 'grim' financial situation. In 1945 external aid, mainly from the USA, was enabling Britain to over-spend her income from abroad by £2,100 million. Dalton estimated that it would be 1949 at the earliest before the external account was in balance, and this was on the most favourable assumptions about rising exports. In the meantime, Britain was clearly in need of foreign aid unless it was willing to devalue the pound, cut imports, or massively reduce foreign spending, mainly defence. The first of these options would have imported inflation and probably not increased exports greatly because of production difficulties; the second option would have meant massive cuts in living standards; and the third could not produce rapid advantages because of problems in running down commitments (as well as raising the questions about the need for defence expenditure).

In the event, the government chose to try to negotiate a free loan from America, though at the same time making defence economies.[34] The government was encouraged in this decision by Keynes, who was the chief British negotiator for the loan. Initially he was confident that a loan of £1.5 billion could be obtained easily, even as a free gift.[35] But the mood in the American Congress was not one of generosity to the country which, Keynes claimed, had given so much for the Allied effort. The American negotiators made it clear that the deal would have to be a commerical transaction to pass through Congress. Trade and financial conditions were also demanded, notably the ratification of the 1944 Bretton Woods Convention, which sought to limit bilateral and restrictionist policies, and in particular making sterling freely convertible within a year.

This led to a series of major debates in the Cabinet. Many were unhappy about Britain's ability to repay the loan, or fulfil the convertibility demand. Some remembered that in the early stages of the war America had forced Britain to sell off many of her most lucrative assets and buy materials on a cash-and-carry basis, and that now America was demanding conditions which mainly harmed Britain, namely by outlawing preference, but not tariffs. Bevan and Shinwell especially were opposed. Bevan on 6 November argued that America would be forced to help Britain for trade and military reasons; he further believed that many British people would accept massive cuts in living standards; both were debatable claims. Shinwell on 29 November argued that the terms were inimical to the planned economy; he suggested seeking a loan at higher rates, but with no ties. Outside the Cabinet, prominent Labour supporters like Cole advocated breaking off negotiations, especially because it would force the government to take a more positive approach to planning.[36]

The Cabinet baulked at such suggestions. Bevin on 6 November stated that he was reluctant to accept proposals that made 'us subject to economic direction from the United States', but felt there was no other choice. On 29 November he stated that a loan without ties was unobtainable; he further argued that American aid was needed generally throughout Europe. Dalton seemed in a state of panic, envisaging a standard of living for the British people 'less than an Irish peasant', a 'dark valley of austerity' in which the Conservatives would mercilessly exploit Labour's plight. Many could not help but remember that external financial problems had helped bring down the last Labour government, and were loath to court disaster again. Even so, the opposition to the Americans' terms was strong.

In early December the Americans made some small concessions, though still demanding interest, and the convertibility of sterling. The Americans argued that convertibility would be a possibility in view of the credit which was being offered. Part of the Bretton Woods accords also involved the setting up of an International Monetary Fund, which offered the prospect of further loans in the future; and the requirement of fixed exchanges rates appealed as Britain had suffered from competitive devaluations in the inter-war years. A hastily convened Cabinet on 5 December was still less than sure about these terms. However, Keynes was pressing acceptance on Dalton, and the Chancellor urged a settlement. Some in the Cabinet, notably Attlee and Cripps, believed that the agreement was unworkable, but thought that it was better to accept the terms and renegotiate later, than become involved in protracted dealings, or go it alone. The terms were therefore accepted.

The American loan agreement provided a $3.75 billion loan (plus $650 million to pay for goods in transit) at 2 per cent interest, repayable over fifty years, payments beginning in 1951. The acceptance of Bretton Woods and the convertibility of sterling within a year of ratification were included in the terms of the agreement. An additional loan of $1,250 million was made by the Canadian government on the same basis. Later in December Parliament approved the agreement, and on 15 July 1946 President Truman signed legislation authorising the loan, after a long debate in Congress which showed that many in the USA were far from sympathetic to external commitments, or helping a Labour-governed Britain.

The relationship between Britain's internal policy and external events was further highlighted by the food situation in 1946. Britain during the second world war had been a country of shortages, of queues, of rationing, of children chewing carrots instead of sweets, of ersatz foods, and no foods. At the end of the war many people hoped that this would change. But in December 1945 a Gallup poll found that 55 per cent thought that the shortages were greater than the year before; and during 1946 things were to get worse! In February the world war two staple, dried eggs, disappeared completely from the market, victims of the ending of Lend-Lease. No sooner had they reappeared than a bread crisis developed.

The 1946 bread crisis stemmed from several factors. In 1945 there had been a poor world harvest, aggravating a shortage brought about by the war. Some grain had to be diverted to India to alleviate starvation there, and Bevin wanted 150,000 tons of British reserve wheat to be sent to a poverty-stricken British zone in Germany. In April the Ministry of Food decided to reduce the size of loaves, but on 25 May Sir Ben Smith, the Minister of Food, reported to the Cabinet that without rationing there might be bread riots in some places. Smith, an aged trade unionist who had proved a less than efficient minister, was replaced two days later by John Strachey.

Strachey had been appointed Under Secretary for Air in 1945, and had quickly shown that he was an able publicist and efficient administrator, but he was also initially convinced of the need for rationing. The Cabinet confirmed this decision on 27 June, and Strachey issued an order introducing bread rationing on 21 July. As more favourable data came in Strachey began to change his mind. On 18 July he submitted a memorandum to the Cabinet opposing rationing. Morrison, who opposed bread rationing, tried to call an emergency Cabinet while Attlee, Dalton and Bevan were at the Durham Miners' Gala; Attlee postponed the meeting for a day. When the Cabinet met on 21 July it decided to proceed with rationing, a decision which owed as much to personality as rationality: Dalton in particular disliked Strachey, and there was some hostility towards Morrison for attempting to call an emergency Cabinet, though Cripps supported Morrison.[37]

Although subsequently some Labour ministers tried to defend the scheme,[38] it worked badly and probably did Labour harm. When it ended in 1948 there had been little or no grain saving. The Cabinet had never thought that there would be a great saving; the point had been more to ensure an equitable distribution in the event of a deterioration in the situation. Nevertheless, there had been an escalation in the bureaucracy to no obvious effect, and a lot of angry bakers and housewives, annoyed by coupons and forms. On the first day of the working of the scheme, a young Conservative named Edward Heath held Bexley in a by-election with a swing of 11.1 per cent, the highest of any by-election during 1945-1946. It was a bad omen for Labour as Britain's economic position remained a precarious one, and inconvenient for those like Bevan who believed that the British people would have accepted massive cuts in living standards to be independent of the USA.

Part Three: Foreign, Defence and Colonial Policy

In spite of an extensive legislative programme and mounting economic crisis, foreign, defence and colonial policy attracted considerable attention in the Labour Party, if not among the public. The government had to face many major problems. In 1945 Britain was still involved in vast areas of the world — the Far East, Middle East, Europe and elsewhere. It was a rapidly changing world, which was watching the emergence of two new superpowers in the USA and USSR, one of which had atomic weapons, and the other of which would clearly have them soon. It was a world in which Britain's position was circumscribed by complex factors, including her economic position. It was against this background that Labour struggled to decide on Britain's future role.[39]

Bevin as Foreign Secretary undertook coordinating activities in external affairs similar to those which Morrison performed in the domestic field, though there was no Cabinet committee on foreign affairs, and Bevin tended to be a more dominant personality. Only Attlee, who until late 1946 doubled as Minister of Defence, was a major figure among the other ministers concerned with external affairs, and he tended primarily to be interested in domestic policy and general management of the government. Below the ministerial level was a series of departmental committees similar to those in other major fields, including a committee consisting of a junior minister and the Deputy and Assistant Under-Secretaries, which dealt with the task of preparing studies on long-term policy.

Labour's foreign policy bore strong resemblances to that pursued by the wartime coalition. Many at the time, and since, have used this to demonstrate Labour's betrayal of a 'socialist' foreign policy.[40] However, the idea of a 'socialist' foreign policy had always been somewhat vague, often hiding a romantic internationalism, or narrow 'little Englander' mentality, ideas which were of debatable relevance in the post-1945 world. Moreover, it is important to remember that the traditional view that Labour had little to do with the shaping of foreign policy during the war is erroneous.[41] Since the 1930s the party leadership had taken a growing interest in foreign policy, and during the war Labour's concern with post-war reform did not preclude a strong interest in this sphere. The views of the Labour leaders showed similarities throughout this period, combining realism with idealism, though in general realism gained the upper hand, and Labour's policy was in many spheres undoubtedly similar to that which would have been pursued by a Conservative government.

The accusation that Labour betrayed a socialist foreign policy is often linked to the charge that the Foreign Office exerted considerable influence over Bevin. Bevin undoubtedly became devoted to his officials, a somewhat surprising relationship between this essentially working-class man who liked his bottle of 'newts' (*Nuits St Georges*), and his upper-

and middle-class public school-Oxbridge advisers.[42] However, Bevin was a man with strong views on most issues, a man who spoke of 'my' policy; he was not the sort to be led easily, especially as he was an experienced minister. True, after 1945 he became increasingly ill, and less able to work hard, but the main outlines of his policies were decided before he came to office, and in the early days. In the 1930s Bevin had been the the union leader most concerned with foreign policy; he had travelled quite widely as a trade union leader. His interest had been a fairly narrow one, and he was certainly no expert, but Bevin's policy after 1945 can be better understood in terms of his own views than in terms of Foreign Office influence. If at times he espoused what was considered the Foreign Office line, this did not necessarily mean that he had acquired the position from the Foreign Office, though it clearly provided an important environment in which some of his ideas were formed. Similarly, although Bevin maintained secret contacts with the former Tory Foreign Secretary, there is no reason to think that Anthony Eden significantly influenced Bevin.

Certainly the two major questions which concerned Labour on coming to office were ones on which Bevin already held strong views. These were the German settlement, and the international post-war world, especially relations with the USA and USSR, questions which were closely related.

In the 1930s there had been a strong tendency in the Labour Party to differentiate between Germans and Nazis, but this had declined during the war, and Labour sought radical changes in Germany. In particular, Attlee, Bevin, Dalton and others advocated the breaking up of the strong central German government, the dismemberment of the country, the nationalisation of the major industries, and political re-education to create a social democratic state.[43]

Labour in the inter-war years had been internationalist, a supporter of collective security, though many in the party had strong nationalist views.[44] By 1944 there were some doubts in this sphere, especially in view of the failure of the League of Nations. America's absence from the League increased desires to ensure American participation in the post-war world. In 1945 it was not clear that America would resist the appeals of isolationism; some thought she would retreat into fortress America, deserting 'imperialist' Britain and the old world. Many in 1945 hoped for cooperation with the Soviet Union, especially in view of what were seen as the disastrous consequences of ignoring Russia in the late 1930s. But from the outset Attlee doubted whether any serious form of cooperation was possible, an important factor in his decision to appoint Bevin Foreign Secretary. Bevin had never been an admirer of the Soviet Union, and had experienced trouble from communists in his beloved TGWU. Although in 1945 he hoped that cooperation would be possible, he was not as sanguine as Dalton.[45]

The growing fears and tensions between the wartime allies were clear at the Potsdam conference, which met in July-August to consider the European peace treaties. The centrepiece of Potsdam was the future of Germany. It was decided that Germany should be treated uniformly by the four occupying powers, Britain, France, the USA and USSR. Among other decisions were that Germany should in part be de-industrialised, and reparations paid to the victors, although the sum was not fixed. The general aim was to produce a Germany which could never again threaten Europe's peace.

This agreement papered over many cracks between the Allies. Germany rapidly became a major source of division, and a central problem for Britain, pushing her towards the USA and away from the Soviet Union. Miliband has argued that 'even before the Cold War was properly under way' Britain had 'unhesitatingly' taken 'its place as the most senior of the junior partners of the United States'.[46] However, this view ignores the fact that initially Bevin held some hopes of cooperation with the Soviet Union, and fails to take into account the role which Germany played in the ending of 'big three' unity.

The British occupation zone in Germany was badly devastated, desperately in need of aid, particularly food. In spite of this, the Russians refused to supply food from their more agricultural zone; almost certainly the Russians were happy to see the Germans starve, especially when eastern Europe needed food. In the absence of food from the Soviet zone, Britain was forced to supply large quantities of aid. In May 1946, with bread rationing imminent in Britain, 75,000 tons of wheat was sent to a starving British zone; the Cabinet decided not to publicise this fact in Britain. In July the Americans were informed that the British were spending £100 million per annum above military costs, and could not afford it!

In the same month Bevin told the Cabinet that he had agreed to an American plan to merge the British and American zones. He accepted that this risked dividing Europe in two, but argued that this might have a 'salutary' effect on the USSR; he added that there was nothing in the agreement to prevent the Soviet Union (and France) joining in as well, and that British plans for socialising industries would not be affected. Bevin reported that problems extended beyond economic aid. The Russians (and French) were demanding industrial reparations from the British zone, a policy which threatened to make it a further burden on Britain.

In April 1946 the Soviet occupying authorities had forced a merger of the communists and social democrats in their zone. The Soviet Union seemed intent on eliminating forces hostile to its interests, as it had done elsewhere, notably in Poland. Bevin further presented an intelligence report which claimed that the Russians were also breaking the Potsdam agreement by using the German war machine to manufacture arms, including rockets!

In March 1946 at Fulton, Missouri, Churchill made a well publicised speech claiming that an 'iron curtain' was descending between east and western Europe. This speech justifiably attracted considerable criticism in the Labour Party for being provocative and potentially self-fulfilling. Bevin clearly dissociated himself and the government from the statement. However, although in the early days of the government there had been frequent references in Cabinet about the need not to isolate the Soviet Union, by late 1945 Bevin had growing doubts about the possibilities of cooperation. In January 1946 he warned the Cabinet that the Soviet Union was making territorial demands, including former Italian colonies, and was occupying part of Iran. There were further troubles over the European peace treaties, and over the settlement in the Far East.

Bevin's growing hostility to the Soviet Union met with some opposition, notably from Dalton and Bevan. Dalton argued that the Soviet Union had many legitimate fears and needs, and that it was important not to isolate her by taking a completely hostile line. In particular, he thought that a more sympathetic attitude might be taken over reparations in view of the horrifying destruction which the war had wreaked on Russia. Bevan rejected the view that the Soviet Union was expansionist or a threat to the peace, and further argued against close ties with the Americans. However, within the Cabinet these increasingly became minority views as 1946 progressed.[47]

Nevertheless, outside the Cabinet criticism of the government's foreign policy began to grow. Within the Labour Party there was a small pacifist group which seemed opposed to any foreign policy. There was a larger group of fellow travellers, even covert communists, who were uncritically pro-Soviet. Many of these were to be found on the backbench Foreign Affairs Committee, one reason why Bevin consulted it far less often than Dalton consulted the Economics Committee. There was additionally a growing section of the party which was neither pacifist, nor fellow traveller, but which disliked Bevin's foreign policy. In November 1946 Labour backbenchers tabled an amendment to the Address which called for a 'genuinely Socialist foreign policy' to provide a 'democratic and constructive alternative to an otherwise inevitable conflict between American capitalism and Soviet Communism'. Forty-four members originally tabled the amendment, and although government pressure resulted in no Labour MP voting for the amendment when pushed to a divison by two ILP members, *The Times* estimated that one hundred and twenty-two Labour MPs abstained. The party seemed on the verge of taking up where it had left off in the late 1930s — dividing badly over foreign policy.

The critics might have gained greater support had the United Nations offered a more serious possibility as an international peace-keeping organisation. The draft charter of the UN had been signed in San Francisco in June 1945. Attlee, Bevin and most Labour leaders welcomed the new organisation. In Cabinet in September 1945 it was stated that the UN must take up the role of defending British interests, though it was accepted that it would not be a viable organisation for some time. In a discussion on atomic research during November 1945 Bevin suggested that the UN might be a body to which scientific information relating to war could be given; it was noted that the atomic bomb was already causing tensions in USA-USSR relations, and it was agreed that Britain should try to act as a mediator. In January 1946 Attlee told the House of Commons that the UN must become the overriding factor in foreign policy. Many others hoped that the UN would offer the institutional format for cooperation with the Soviet Union, or provide an internationalist position, separate from the two superpowers. But during 1946 great power squabbles were transferred to the UN itself. And, like the ill-fated League of Nations, it did not have any armed forces in its own right. This seemed particularly important to the British government in the new atom age, and when Britain was trying to make large defence economies.

Britain at the end of the war demobilised fairly quickly. It could probably have proceeded slightly more quickly, but at the Cabinet meeting of 16 August Bevin requested that it was important not to give the impression that Britain was demobilising too quickly in view of the international position, and other ministers feared temporary unemployment if demobilisation was too rapid. Nevertheless, at the end of the war Britain had 5,100,000 men and women in the forces; by December 1946 this figure had fallen to 1,000,000.

This was still a large number by inter-war standards, and defence expenditure at £1,653 million in 1946, a fifth of gross national product, was high compared to the inter-war average.[48] Naturally, this was the subject of considerable criticism within the party. However, there were vivid memories in the leadership of the lack of British defence preparations in the 1930s, which militated against too rapid a run-down of forces in a world which seemed far from stable. There were strong fears about Soviet intentions; there were further doubts about America's commitment to a world role. Even so, Dalton in Cabinet on 28 September 1945 called for a cutting of defence expenditure to £500 million, and Attlee and Bevin agreed that large cuts were necessary. Presenting the defence budget in Cabinet in February 1946 Attlee claimed that the cuts involved 'considerable risks'; Bevin even requested that the extent of the cuts for 1947 should not be made public – his trade union training had taught him the value of power, and negotiating from a position of apparent strength. There is no question of the fact that the government was trying to make large defence cuts, in part a reflection of economic necessity and hoped-for American cooperation, but also as a result of withdrawal from India and other traditional spheres of British influence.

Indian independence was the only specific colonial policy promised in *Let Us Face the Future*; colonial policy had never been a major concern in the party, though there was an active minority interested in the field.[49] For other 'colonial dependencies' there was to be 'planned progress'. Behind this vague statement lay three main attitudes. First, there was a not unreasonable belief that economic and social development had to precede independence, and that the minority which would probably rule after independence was far more worrying than 'benevolent' British rule. This view had some ethnocentric aspects, and a more general argument of this type involved a racial typology which saw African countries especially as less fitted for self-government. Finally, there were some fears, mainly in the union wing of the party, about the economic effects on prices and employment in Britain, a reflection of a social imperialist perspective.

Nevertheless, it would be wrong to overstate the economic side of British policy, as many have done.[50] During the American loan negotiations the Americans pressed for a reduction in Britain's sterling balances with colonial countries. George Hall, the Colonial Secretary, told the Cabinet that this would be politically impossible, and there was a strong feeling in the party that it would be morally wrong to renege on debts to poor countries. In general, Labour tried hard to wind up parts of the old Empire, and during 1945-1946 efforts were made particularly over Indian independence, though in a period of considerable legislative activity, and economic and foreign problems, colonial policy was inevitably not a major concern for the party or Cabinet.

Chapter Five

'ANNUS HORRENDUS', 1947

'Attlee and Co. have handled this crisis very badly, both politically and psychologically.'

H. Laski to F. Frankfurter, 29 May 1947. Letter in D. Woodman Papers.

Part One: Economic Policy

For Dalton 1946 was *'Annus Mirabilis'*, the year in which Sir Hartley Shawcross really should have said 'We are the masters now.' 1947 was *'Annus Horrendus'*, the year in which everything seemed to go wrong. the year in which the Conservatives, who had been in disarray during 1945-1946, found renewed confidence — and overtook Labour in public opinion polls.[1]

The year began with the worst winter of the century. On 5 January it began to snow in most places, and it went on, and on, until by late January most of the country was paralysed. Added to the inevitable problems this brought in its wake was a coal crisis.

On 1 January 1947 the coal industry had become a state industry. This was a working day, and so it was on 5 January that the miners gathered in the pits, often with their families, to celebrate the 'salvation' of nationalisation: plaques were unveiled, bands played, it was just like a holiday! But production in the mines was low, a reflection of problems during the transition to peacetime and nationalisation. As early as 24 June 1946 the Cabinet had discussed a Morrison memorandum which pointed to the critical nature of coal stocks; Shinwell, who was planning to introduce a five-day week for the miners, assured the Cabinet that the situation was under control. By late 1946 production was indeed rising, but so was demand as industrial output began to pick up.

By the beginning of January it was clear that a crisis was developing. Cripps produced a plan to allocate the limited coal resources, but this was overtaken by the weather, which was so bad that what coal there was often could not be moved. The Cabinet was beginning to panic; it seriously discussed whether to stop the installation of electric appliances, and to allow cooking only at certain times of the day! On 6 February it rejected a proposal from Shinwell to impose power cuts, but on the following day Shinwell claimed that 'drastic' cuts were necessary as a result of low coal reserves at the generating stations, and the Cabinet agreed. The resulting cuts added to the dislocation.[2]

Unemployment on 9 December 1946 had totalled 362,976, or nearly 2.1 per cent. At its peak in February it reached 1,916,000 on the register, and an estimated 503,200 unregistered — 15.5 per cent. By March things were slowly returning to normal as the weather eased, but the crisis had been a traumatic one for Labour. Dalton noted in his diary on 12 March that it had broken the 'morale of all of us'. At the same time, the Conservatives began to gain confidence, producing the famous slogan 'Starve with Strachey and shiver with Shinwell.' There was a certain irony in their claim that more planning could have averted the crisis, and the argument that the problem stemmed from nationalisation missed the point that in late 1946 production was rising. Nevertheless, the crisis provided the Conservatives with excellent material to attack Labour.

The loss of production as a result of the crisis was serious, possibly costing as much as £200 million in exports. This added to a worsening balance of payments situation. There was a seller's market, and British exports did well during 1945-1946, but the imbalance with the hard currency areas remained massive. Of the $3,750 million American loan, $600 million had been used up by the end of 1946, and another $500 million went up to April 1947. Additionally, the terms of trade were worsening against Britain, a trend which was to add over £300 million to the import bill in 1947. These were hardly good omens for the convertibility of sterling, which under the terms of the American loan agreement would come into effect in July 1947.

During early 1947 the Cabinet spent considerable time discussing Britain's economic problems. Particular attention was paid to the 'manpower gap'. On 16 January the Cabinet discussed what could be done about labour in non-productive enterprises, like football pools. It discussed the 'conscription' of women between 18 and 20 to work in important industries; the Minister of Labour disingenuously argued that this would mean greater equality (there was military conscription for men). More seriously, Dalton launched a major assault on defence spending, including the number of men in the services, and related industries. Cuts were agreed, with resulting savings of foreign currency, but the Cabinet in general showed a reluctance to consider Britain's external financial situation. As early as 16 January Cripps had pointed to the dangers of the balance of payments position; on 27 March Dalton warned of the 'alarming rate at which' the American credit was being exhausted. Dalton followed this up on 5 June with a call for cuts in imports, including food imports. This was strongly backed especially by Cripps, but nothing was agreed. In part this reflected a failure to perceive the seriousness of the situation, but there were other fears about the impact of such cuts. Strachey told the Cabinet that since the war there had been a 'substantial deterioration in our diet, which was now physiologically inadequate for those sections of the population who had no access to canteens or differential rations'. Nevertheless, on 24 June the Cabinet agreed to some cuts.

On 15 July the pound became convertible. Initially there was nothing approaching a run on sterling, though the conversion rate was high. Britain had already been forced to accept that the Argentine and Canada could convert some of their current sales, and the situation was made worse by a general world shortage of dollars. On 29 July Dalton informed the Cabinet that the American loan would run out by October, possibly in September. On 1 August he told the Cabinet that there was a need for widespread import cuts, including luxury foods, 'such as canned fruit'. The previous night Attlee, Bevin, Cripps, Dalton and Morrison had met to discuss the situation. Attlee seemed bewildered; Bevin was drunk; Morrison left in disgust; and Dalton soldiered on by taking Benzedrine. The government was living on its nerves rather than its wits.

The Cabinet on 1 August agreed to an austerity programme, which was made public on 6 August. The miners were to work an extra half hour a day, food imports from hard currency areas were reduced by £12 million, the basic petrol ration was reduced; other savings included a 75 per cent tax on American films (the following day the Americans replied by placing an embargo on films to Britain). On 16 August Churchill confirmed Dalton's fears during the American loan negotiations of the Conservatives exploiting external difficulties when he broadcast on the radio, predicting still lower standards of living, and the death or dispersal of a large part of the population. The Conservative press carried equally alarmist reports.

By this time there was a serious loss of confidence in Britain's ability to maintain convertibility, and a run on the pound had started. On 17 August Dalton reported to the Cabinet that there was an accelerating drain on dollars. Drawings in the five days to 15 August had been $175.9 million, compared to an estimate of $150 million for the whole of the second half of August. It was agreed that convertibility would have to be suspended on 19 August, though this was subsequently postponed by a day in order to secure American agreement. By this time $3.6 billion of the $5 billion granted by the USA and Canada had been expended![3] On 23 August the government announced further cuts in the meat ration, and the abolition of the basic petrol ration; public dinners were restricted, and foreign travel for pleasure purposes was suspended. It had been a traumatic month for Labour!

Many at the time, and since, have criticised the government's handling of the situation. Certainly Dalton had great difficulty in persuading his colleagues of the necessity for cuts in overseas expenditure. Many failed fully to appreciate the external dimension in economic policy; others thought that increased exports could solve the problem; some saw the difficulties in making cuts, especially in food imports. Furthermore, the government made no serious effort to negotiate the running down of sterling balances, which accounted for a large part of the capital out-flow during July-August, though in the case of poor countries, like India, which was suffering from mass starvation, it was difficult to deny them funds so that Britain could consume more. Some in the government, notably Cripps, seem almost to have welcomed the crisis as a means of achieving a *de facto* renegotiation of the American loan; a formal re-negotiation was unquestionably impossible, but the manner of ending convertibility was damaging to the government. The point here is more a political than an economic one, a fact missed by many critics.[4]

The American loan of 1945 had given the government time to under-take certain economic policies, and to educate the people to Britain's problems. The government made some efforts to explain the economic situation, but in general it failed to convey an accurate picture of Britain's economic position to home opinion. People were aware that there were serious problems, but they did not fully understand the causes of these troubles. Labour's propaganda was essentially negative, appealing for harder work and more production. At the same time, Labour's complacent statements about convertibility earlier in 1947 had little effect on inter-national confidence, though they served to increase the shock domestically when convertibility was suspended and the austerity programme announced. The cuts appeared to be the result of imcompetence rather than necessity or part of a plan.

Mounting economic crisis was accompanied by growing attacks on Attlee's leadership, particularly the lack of direction in economic policy, and his inability to inspire the electorate. Cripps and Dalton were the central figures in this plotting. Both were genuinely worried by Attlee's leadership, though Cripps also hoped to gain advancement through a change, and Dalton was an inveterate conspirator: it was said that if he had ever become leader he would have started plotting against himself! During July Dalton tried to persuade Bevin to accept the leadership.[5] Bevin told Dalton that he found Attlee weak, and that he wanted more trade union men in the Cabinet. But he was not keen to replace Attlee; he was preoccupied with work at the Foreign Office, and still retained a strong sense of loyalty. A similar approach by both Cripps and Dalton on 17 August met with a further rebuff.

On 5 September Cripps told Dalton that he was considering resigning over the issue, but first wanted to try to persuade Morrison to come in on the plot. Morrison still thought of himself as a potential leader, though among leading colleagues his stock had fallen. He talked too much in Cabinet and on committees, seeking a finger in every pie. His economic capabilities were under attack, and there were doubts about his health. As early as April Cripps was telling Dalton that Morrison was incapable of planning and that Bevin must take over. Morrison had additionally just burned his fingers over an attempt to negotiate a compromise with the iron and steel owners over nationalisation, a mission undertaken at Attlee's suggestion!

Cripps's approach to Morrison was therefore a hopeful one to put it mildly. Morrison was being asked to support the elevation of Bevin, whom he hated, while his own economic role was taken away. Cripps's meeting with Morrison produced the predictable result. Morrison agreed that Attlee needed replacing, but suggested himself instead. On the following day Morrison saw Dalton, clearly worried by these developments, and stated that if there was to be a change it should be decided by the PLP — a strictly constitutional position, though as over his attitude in 1945, one which promised to favour him.[6]

On 9 September Cripps, hardly showing the 'loyalty to Mr Attlee which was proof against the recurrent waves of criticism of the Prime Minister' claimed by C.A. Cooke,[7] visited Attlee and told him of his desire to see Bevin Prime Minister, with strong powers as an economic overlord. He suggested that Attlee should become Chancellor of the Exchequer, Dalton Foreign Secretary, and himself Lord Privy Seal. Attlee was well aware of the mounting criticism, and responded adroitly. He accepted Cripps's criticisms of the problems in economic management, and claimed that these could be resolved by Cripps taking over the top economic job as Minister for Economic Affairs, a post which Cripps accepted. Attlee had again proved that there was a wily fox inside the sheep's clothing.

Attlee's appointment of Cripps to an overseeing role in economic coordination reflected more than just an attempt to silence his criticism. Increasingly since 1945 it had become clear that Labour's economic planning was neither coherent, nor well coordinated.

In February 1947 there had appeared the first Economic Survey of the government. It talked of collecting information to assess national resources and needs, of 'economic budgets' to relate these needs to resources. It set specific targets for manpower and output in certain industries, and presented a comprehensive import programme. But for all the talk of planning, Labour's proposals were still essentially piecemeal, dealing with general aspirations like restricting domestic demand and making scarce materials available for export industries. The Survey itself argued that there were limits to planning, claiming that 'the task of directing by democratic methods an economic system as large and complex as ours is far beyond the power of any Government machine.' Donoughue and Jones have criticised Morrison for the problems in planning, for his lack of economic expertise, 'flair', or 'feel',[8] but in part the troubles stemmed from a long-standing vagueness of policy, and the lack of any serious discussion of the relationship between democracy and planning.

Nevertheless, coordination was not that effective, in spite of Morrison's supposed activities in this field through his Lord President's Committee. This resulted in the decision to appoint an inter-departmental planning staff, under a Chief Planning Officer, who was a director of British Aluminium and two other companies. This was designed to develop long-term plans for the country's resources, and to improve contacts between the Lord President's Office and other departments. However, the appointment of Cripps as Minister of Economic Affairs meant that the Lord President's Committee lost its economic planning role, this function passing mainly to the Economic Policy Committee under Attlee. Cripps's new department was given the Economic Planning Staff, together with the Economic Information Unit and the Economic Section of the Cabinet Office, but the Treasury remained separate. This new arrangement threatened further coordination problems until in November 1947 Dalton resigned as Chancellor of the Exchequer. His replacement was Cripps, who took with him his various advisers, as the office of Minister of Economic Affairs was merged with the Exchequer.

In November 1947 Dalton presented his second budget of the year. In his first budget he had announced a prospective surplus of £248 million, compared to a deficit of £569 million for 1946-1947, the main change coming from reduced defence expenditure, though taxes in general were raised, and a special Profits Tax was introduced which discriminated against distributed profits. In October Dalton announced cuts in investment as part of the austerity programme; the November budget included cuts in subsidies, and increases in purchase tax and profits tax. On the way to make his speech Dalton had spoken briefly to the lobby correspondent of the *Star*. Parts of his speech appeared in the paper before the relevant part of the speech was delivered. Dalton had always been known for talking too much; it was said that if he had been appointed Foreign Secretary he would have ended secret diplomacy! His indiscretion on this occasion was to cost him dear, for he was forced to resign.[9]

Dalton's indiscretion was in many ways a lucky one for the government, which had need of a scapegoat after the economic troubles of 1947. Cripps was ideally suited to Labour's austerity programme. Gone was his left-wing radicalism of the early 1930s. During the late 1930s he had become interested in Keynesian economics, and disillusioned with the radical potential of the working class, points missed by commentators who focus on his attitude towards Russia in the second world war.[10] Nevertheless, he had retained strong religious views and his messianic style. These could now be used to preach the need for further austerity, a sermon which well suited the ascetic life style of Britain's new Chancellor of the Exchequer.[11]

Already on 7 August, while still President of the Board of Trade, he had shown during the 'State of the Nation' debate in the House of Commons a remarkable facility for rousing appeals to both sides of industry. He demanded greater production, more exports, and the acceptance of hardships. As Chancellor he was to excel himself in his ability for expressing intense passion in demanding harder work. Giant posters in the street exhorted 'We're up against it! We WORK or WANT.' Exactly how much influence these appeals had is not clear, but British industrial production unquestionably rose rapidly at this time. From an index of 146 in 1938 (1924=100), production rose to 149 by 1946, 159 by 1947, and 172 in 1948, though other factors were clearly important in this growth.

However, a case can be made that, although in many ways suited to the time, Cripps as Chancellor of the Exchequer put another nail in Labour's socialist coffin. Cripps retained strong socialist views, albeit of a more Fabian kind. But these tended to be subsumed in his general appeals for production, exports and sacrifices. Labour was increasingly adopting a technocratic economic appeal even before Cripps became Chancellor; Dalton was certainly no socialist proselytiser. Ironically, under Cripps this tendency was carried further. Labour was losing its soul.

Part Two: Foreign, Defence and Colonial Policy

External affairs were increasingly to concern Labour during 1947. The mounting economic crisis had serious effects on Britain's external commitments. At the same time, important developments were taking place which were essentially unrelated to the economic situation. Together they heralded the onset of the cold war, the division of the world into two hostile major camps.

1947 began with the Cabinet discussing a proposal to bring down Franco's hated Spanish government by sanctions. M.R. Gordon has claimed that Labour did nothing to achieve this 'socialist' desire,[12] but the issue had been under consideration since it was raised in Cabinet by Ellen Wilkinson in February 1946. Bevin in a memorandum dated 3 Janaury 1947 pointed out the problems involved in imposing sanctions; in particular, it seemed that the Argentine and USA would not comply. The proposal was therefore rejected; reality overcame idealism.

Immediately after, the Cabinet became engaged in a heated discussion of defence expenditure. Dalton sought major cuts, and concentrated his fire on the British presence in Greece. As a result on 30 January the Cabinet agreed to set up a committee to see what could be done to persuade the USA to give long-term financial, economic and military aid to Greece.

Greece and the eastern Mediterranean had long been an area of British interest, particularly after its purchase of the Suez canal shares, and later the discovery of oil in Arab states. British troops had occupied Greece as the Germans retreated in the second world war. Churchill in 1944 had come to a deal with Stalin which made Greece a British sphere of influence, though this did not prevent an attempted communist coup, and later Soviet efforts to push Britain out. British presence was therefore linked with an attempt to promote a friendly government, which in practice meant a fairly right-wing one. This policy was strongly attacked at the 1944 Labour conference. Subsequently, Greece continued to prove a troublesome issue for the Labour government, though Bevin tried hard to claim that his policy was in line with the 1944 Labour conference policy, and he sought to protect the non-communist Greek left.[13]

These troubles encouraged Attlee to think of withdrawing from at least part of the eastern Mediterranean. On the other hand, Bevin was becoming more and more convinced of the need to remain in order to protect British interests, and resist Soviet expansion. The Chiefs of Staff were also keen to remain. This led to a major crisis in early 1947, with Dalton threatening to resign if Britain did not cut back her defence commitments, and the Chiefs of Staff threatening to resign if Britain made such a move. The result was an attempt to persuade the United States to accept responsibilities in the eastern Mediterranean, a policy which fitted in with Bevin's general desire to prevent a return to American isolationism, and fears of Soviet desires to secure a permanent position in this area.

On 12 March 1947 in a momentous move President Truman approached Congress and asked for a $400 million grant to aid Greece and Turkey resist the communist threat! Britain had been relieved of her commitments in these countries, but the inflammatory nature of Truman's appeal to Congress helped reinforce the division which was taking place between east and west (and reflected the fact that American desire for external commitments was far from certain!).

Three months later a further American move made the iron curtain even stronger. On 5 June the Secretary of State, George Marshall, put forward tentative proposals to aid Europe's economic plight. In the following week it was stated that this offer included the Soviet Union, but this offer was diplomatic rather than serious. Certainly Bevin, who responded to the speech with alacrity, saw the offer essentially in western European terms. On 17 June he informed the Cabinet that he had sent a message to the Soviet Union stressing that the Marshall plan only covered economic aims, but he argued that Britain should go ahead even without Soviet cooperation. Some have argued that Bevin only finally accepted the reality of the cold war after the Soviet Union's response to the Marshall offer.[14] In fact, although Bevin was still expressing in Cabinet hopes of agreement on a united Germany, he had long since despaired of achieving any serious form of cooperation with the Soviet Union.

The Soviet Union replied to Marshall aid with the formation of the Cominform, and by instructions to western communist parties to cease cooperation with non-communists. At the inaugural meeting of the Cominform the world was proclaimed to be divided irrevocably into two camps. This seemed to reflect Soviet policy elsewhere. During 1947 Russia consolidated communist domination in eastern Europe, and in February 1948 communists in Czechoslovakia carried out a *coup* which brought down the last relatively independent government in eastern Europe.

Within three years the wartime cooperation of the great powers had turned into hostility. Many have sought to analyse this development in terms of, on the one hand, Soviet expansionism, or, on the other hand, American hostility to communism. Others have focused on the decline of Britain, and her role, especially in seeking an American commitment to the old world.[15] There is an element of truth in each of these perspectives, but the cold war cannot be analysed easily: it was the result of complex pressures and responses. Almost certainly it could not have been avoided. Moreover, a concentration on post-1945 disunity is in some ways misleading; wartime cooperation was the unusual situation.

Many in the Labour Party did not see the origins of the cold war in these terms. At the 1947 Labour conference there were fierce attacks on the pamphlet, *Cards on the Table*, written by a young Transport House assistant, Dennis Healey. This in effect called for an Anglo-American front against the Soviet menace. Critics claimed Labour's policy was essentially Tory: as one backbench wit said of Bevin, 'Hasn't Anthony Eden grown fat!' M.R. Gordon has written that 'The rank and file, together with a large, probably overwhelming, majority of backbench MPs, approached the post-war era fully convinced that their leaders would proceed to implement a socialist foreign policy.'[16] The symbol of socialism undoubtedly remained important in maintaining the Labour coalition. Nevertheless, it is important not to overstate the opposition to Bevin's policy, and to realise that the critics were badly divided over an alternative. Moreover, both Bevin and his foreign policy were highly rated in public opinion polls; criticism within the Labour Party was not mirrored by popular feeling.

One group of critics was the pacifists, a group for whom Bevin had nothing but contempt, as his brutal destruction of George Lansbury at the 1935 Labour conference had shown. Bevin considered the fellow travellers naive, or disingenuous; their argument that as the Soviet Union was not capitalist, it could be neither expansionist nor imperialist, he considered was completely divorced from reality. Although Bevin did not believe that Stalin specifically sought war, the cabinet papers for 1947 and 1948 show clearly that he feared Soviet expansion in the face of western weakness. Bevin rejected the portrayal of the United States as 'capitalist'; he sought to stress the possibilities of Anglo-American democracy, of the 'special relationship'.

Another group of critics centred around Richard Crossman, Ian Mikardo and Michael Foot. In May 1947 this group issued the famous *Keep Left* manifesto. This criticised Britain's relationship with 'capitalist' America, and hostility to the Soviet Union. It proposed closer collaboration with Europe and the Commonwealth. It offered a 'Third Force' position, an attempt to create a block of countries which was neither in the communist nor in the capitalist camp. In late 1946 and early 1947 it offered the most serious of the alternative positions, particularly in view of the socialist, or partly socialist, governments in many leading European and some Commonwealth countries. Bevin briefly was attracted to the idea, but rejected it because he put great emphasis on the economic and military weakness of the European countries; alone they were in no position to resist the Soviet Union. For them to be a serious force in the short run in anything other than 'moral' terms would require increased British defence expenditure, and most critics were hostile to this!

Dalton's efforts to reduce generally military expenditure in early 1947 had run into serious opposition in the Cabinet. Attlee pointed to the 'disastrous' effects of reducing arms expenditure after the first world war, and Bevin pointed to the dangers of the world situation. However, Dalton received strong support from Cripps and others who were impressed by the economic arguments in favour of cuts. By 21 January the defence estimates had been cut from £913 million to £822 million. Dalton demanded a further cut to £750 million for 1947-1948. This was opposed by the Minister of Defence, A.V. Alexander, who had succeeded Attlee in this post in December 1946, and by the Chiefs of Staff, but on 28 January a compromise was reached on a further cut of 5 per cent. After the convertibility crisis, Attlee announced more cuts.

While the discussion was proceeding over defence cuts, the decision was taken to spend £140 million over seven years on the construction of a British atomic bomb, expenditure that was carefully concealed in the supply estimates.[17] C.J. Bartlett has argued that the final decision on this was taken in the spring of 1948 in the face of the deteriorating defence and world position.[18] In fact, the important decision had been taken in January 1947. The service chiefs were pressing strongly for a British bomb, and American obduracy in supplying the bomb, or its secrets, encouraged Attlee to press ahead. Indeed, the whole atomic policy was closely supervised by Attlee, and some have seen it as an excellent example of Prime Ministerial power. Certainly, it was not a Cabinet decision, but the preparatory work was done in a committee, and the Cabinet was aware of the decision well before it was made public in a brief statement to the House of Commons in May 1948.

The production of the bomb would clearly take time, and defence strategy in the short run was therefore based on more traditional grounds. During 1946 there was a growing belief in the need to extend conscription after the 1939 act expired in 1949. In November Attlee announced to the

PLP that national service was to be extended, and that the period of service would be eighteen months. This led to considerable criticism, and when the bill was introduced in March 1947 72 MPs voted against it, while 76 abstained. As a result, the period of service was reduced to twelve months. J.P. Mackintosh has argued that this was 'The one occasion on which back-bench opinion influenced the government on an important matter.'[19] However, the central issue, the principle of peacetime conscription, was unaffected, and although the Chiefs of Staff preferred an eighteen-month period, the Chief of the Imperial General Staff, Field Marshall Montgomery, informed the Minister of Defence in April 1947 that a reduction to twelve months would be possible if Britain had no commitments in India and Palestine.

Increasingly after the first world war pressures had grown in India for independence. Labour had long been committed to self-government for India, and had promised this in *Let Us Face the Future*. Nevertheless, the problems the Labour government faced were serious, especially as a result of growing divisions between the 250 million Hindus and 90 million Moslems.[20]

In the spring of 1946 a Cabinet mission visited India. The mission sought to impose a three-tier structure, providing a top tier that would unite the country for purposes of defence and foreign policy, but this policy was rejected. After further negotiations with the Hindu and Moslem leaders, Attlee, strongly backed by Cripps, decided to appoint Lord Mountbatten Viceroy. Attlee and Mountbatten were convinced that Britain needed to set a definite date for withdrawal. In February 1947 it was announced that Britain would withdraw by June 1948 at the latest. Mountbatten arrived on the subcontinent in March. He quickly realised that a solution involving a united India was impossible. Instead, he accepted a plan to partition the country. This was accepted by the Cabinet, and a bill embodying independence along these lines was quickly passed. Mountbatten was keen that the bill should pass unanimously, and approached opposition leaders in Britain to make sure that there was no backwoods Conservative attack, for commitment to the Indian link remained strong in the Tory Party.

The date fixed for withdrawal was 15 August 1947. This was duly kept. Labour had given India her independence.

Left-wing critics at the time, and subsequently, have tried to argue that Britain was forced out of India by a mutiny in the navy and obvious loss of control, that Britian divided the country to keep it weak.[21] These criticisms have little force. The party had long been committed to independence, the government tried hard to elicit Indian opinion, and partition was a necessity in a badly divided country. A more valid criticism would be the speed with which Britain left. The handing over of rule was accompanied by massive population transfers between the new India and Pakistan, and horrifying massacres. Some troubles were inevitable, but had Britain stayed on until the original 1948 date it might have been possible to prevent the worst excesses, to allow a more gradual transfer. However, Bevin was keen to impress on the USA and USSR that 'imperialist' Britain was not delaying her departure. And there was a feeling that the pressure imposed by an early date would help produce a sense of responsibility among Indian leaders. Even so, a slightly less hasty departure would have been preferable.

Britain also decided in 1947 to withdraw from Palestine, which had been a British Mandate since the end of the first world war.[22] In the 1917 Balfour Declaration Britain had promised to set up a national home for the Jews, but the presence of Britain in the Middle East was conditioned by other factors — especially the Suez canal and oil; Britain had also undertaken commitments to the Arabs. During the inter-war years therefore, British governments had strictly limited the inflow of Jews so as not to antagonise Arab opinion.

Jewish settlement in Palestine, with generous compensation for the Arabs, was included in a Labour statement in 1944. However, in October 1945 the Cabinet refused a request from the Jewish Agency, backed by President Truman, for 100,000 entry permits. It was argued in Cabinet that such a policy would lead to an explosion, and would not solve the problem of the Jewish refugees in Europe. Furthermore, there were traditional economic and strategic pressures, heightened at this time by fears of Soviet expansion. Added to these factors was a refusal by Attlee to accept that the Jews were a national group, that they had a right to Palestine, and a belief by Bevin that he could solve the problem. Indeed, Bevin told the House of Commons that he staked his reputation on reaching a solution — a reflection of a trade union belief that all demands are bargainable. There was additionally some hostility to what was seen as American interference.

Nevertheless, later in October the Cabinet decided to invite the American government to join with Britain in setting up a Commission of Enquiry into Palestine. It was hoped that this Commission would see British difficulties, but when it reported in April 1946 it renewed the demand for 100,000 entry permits, though it supported the continuation of the Mandate. This request was again rejected, and during late 1946 the British government tried to achieve a settlement against a background of mounting Jewish terrorism, American pressure, and criticism in the Labour Party, which contained a large pro-Zionist lobby, together with many who sympathised with the Jews as a result of Nazi genocide.

During early 1947 Bevin tried hard to reach agreement with Arab and Jewish leaders over a plan for self-governing Jewish 'cantons' within a predominantly Arab state. He considered partition, which was strongly pushed by Dalton and others, a desperate remedy; he believed that Zionist ultra-nationalism and the pressures of population expansion would make a Jewish state a permanent threat to the Middle East's peace. However, this policy was rejected by both sides, and on 14 February the Cabinet decided to hand the issue over to the UN. This was strongly opposed by the Chiefs of Staff, who saw Palestine as an ideal British base, but although it has been claimed by Miliband that when there were such military-government differences it was 'not the Service Chiefs who had the worst of the encounter',[23] on this occasion they failed. On 31 August a UN Special Committee recommended that the British Mandate should end at the earliest date, and that Palestine should be partitioned. The following month the British government announced that it would withdraw in May 1948, a promise duly kept.

The Labour government's policy over Palestine has been strongly criticised. Some have claimed that it was Bevin's greatest failure; others have argued that Britain should have granted the 100,000 entry visas, that her policy was callous towards a people who had suffered so much, that economic and strategic interests predominated.[24] Bevin undoubtedly failed to produce a peaceful solution; but it is doubtful if such a solution was possible. The government was also influenced by genuine fears about the problems of Jewish immigration, and the future. A more valid criticism would be that Britain again withdrew in a way that heightened the chaos; furthermore, there was an attempt to gain Arab goodwill by supplying arms to some states. The proclamation of the state of Israel in May 1948, followed by its victory in war with the Arabs in 1949, owed nothing to British aid or sympathy.

Part Three: Legislation and Reform

Labour began the 1946-1947 Parliamentary session with another extensive legislative programme, although the experience of the 1945-1946 session led the Future Legislation Committee to make cuts in the original programme because it was clear that even with more widespread use of committees there was a limit to how much Parliament could handle. The economic crisis and growing concern with foreign affairs during 1947 led to further cuts in the domestic programme, notably the delaying of the iron and steel nationalisation bill, though this also stemmed from divisions within the party.

The nationalisation of parts of transport was Labour's major measure during 1946-1947. This was one of Labour's oldest demands; again it was closely connected with pressures from powerful unions, especially the railwaymen and transport workers. It aroused stronger Conservative opposition than any previous Labour measure, with the possible exception of the Trade Disputes and Trade Unions Bill.[25]

During the first and second world wars the railways and canals had been controlled by the government; by 1945 there was growing talk even outside Labour circles of the advantages of nationalisation, particularly because of the need for new investment. In 1945 a substantial part of road transport was already in public hands, notably the London Passenger Transport Board, which had been set up by Morrison during the 1929-1931 government. However, Labour's designs on road haulage were more recent and controversial, although during the war the government had successfully run part of road haulage. Labour further sought to promote a coordinated transport policy. Such a policy was clearly recognised in the 1931 Royal Commission on Transport's report, which had considered nationalisation, but made no firm recommendations.

In spite of growing acceptance of the need to nationalise the railways, the owners proved far less cooperative than the coal owners had been; this was true of the other transport owners. This added to the problems of drafting what was already a complicated bill because of the extent and diversity of the transport industry. On the other hand, the transport unions took a more forceful interest in the development of the bill than the NUM had done with the coal bill. As with mining, Labour in 1945 had no detailed plan for transport nationalisation. This meant that the Minister of Transport, Alfred Barnes, his department, various committees, and the Cabinet were left to work out the details of the bill.[26]

There was general agreement that the railways and canals should be nationalised. The main problems arose over road transport. It was decided not to take over local passenger services. These were usually efficient and did not overcharge; nationalisation might also arouse hostility from the local authorities which ran many of the services. However, the bill provided for coordinating powers to be vested in the new Transport Commission, and for the right to take over services if necessary. A similar provision was made for long-distance services. The difference between long-distance and local services was to be one of the major issues which plagued the planning of road haulage nationalisation. Labour mainly wanted to take over long-distance haulage which was in competition with the railways. This raised a further problem that some long-distance hauliers only carried their own goods. The final draft of the bill contained the somewhat uneasy compromise whereby only long-distance (over forty miles) haulage of others' goods would be nationalised, though there were strict controls on operators who carried only their own goods.

This last aspect was one of the most heavily criticised parts of the bill after it was published in November 1946, especially from industry. Finally, in March 1947 the Cabinet agreed to drop controls on those who carried their own goods. This in turn provoked considerable criticism in the Labour Party, particularly in the Parliamentary Transport Group.

The whole episode points to the problems of nationalising only part of an industry. However, the alternatives would have been even more problematical. Already in October 1945 the minister and Lord President's Committee had ruled out nationalising shipping as adding to the complications of the bill, and prolonging considerably the period before legislation could be introduced. Taking in all road transport would have been far more difficult; at least there was a relatively small number of shipping companies. If there was a lesson here, it was that nationalisation should be avoided when only partial control is concerned unless there is some overriding reason for proceeding; and a sensible gradualist philosophy would probably not rate road transport a very high priority! But then transport nationalisation owed more to union pressure than to any clear gradualist philosophy.

Another aspect of the bill which aroused criticism both from the industry and within the Labour Party was the terms of compensation. The bill did not use the 'net maintainable revenue' formula employed in earlier measures. This system necessarily involved problems over how many years should be used as a base, the distribution of compensation, and so on. As virtually all the railway shares were freely quoted it was decided to base compensation on Stock Exchange prices, with arbitration for shares not quoted. For road haulage, compensation was fixed by accountants and valuers on the basis of the market value of assets, together with other allowances. The railway owners especially criticised the compensation, claiming that quotations were depressed. In truth, compensation was generous, though it is an exaggeration to claim, as Richard Crossman has done, that 'A huge price was paid for a private enterprise on the verge of bankruptcy.'[27]

The second nationalisation measure of the 1946-1947 session was electricity production and supply, another measure vigorously opposed by the Conservatives. The 1936 McGowan Report on the industry had considered nationalisation, though not recommended it. During the war various reorganisation schemes were produced, but the coalition government had failed to reach agreement on a bill for reorganisation. However, Labour's proposals for nationalisation were hardly controversial. The industry was clearly a public service in need of reorganisation; already since the 1920s a Central Electricity Board had acted as a 'wholesaler' to municipal and private undertakings. In 1945 sixty per cent of supply was already in the hands of local authorities; private companies operated mainly under forty-two year charters, and many of these were due to run out in the immediate post-war period. Labour's plan to rest control with a central authority and take over the industry therefore met with little opposition. The main criticism came from local government. There were fears that nationalisation would mean a loss of provision for local needs; and in general local authorities were efficient suppliers. But Fabian municipalisation policies had long since lost favour among intellectuals, and had never had any significant support within the unions. The bill therefore met with little criticism in Parliament. It duly received the Royal Assent on 13 August 1947, seven days after the transport bill.[28]

Another measure which attracted strong Conservative opposition was the 1947 Town and Country Planning Act. The Conservatives opposed in particular the imposition of a 100 per cent levy on the value created by permission to develop land. Addison, in an effort to prove a continuing consensus, had argued that this followed the spirit, if not the letter of the wartime Uthwatt Report.[29] However, this was a controversial issue, and although a 1944 White Paper had suggested an 80 per cent levy, the proposal was allowed to gather dust because of division between the parties. The 1947 act in general brought almost all development land under control by making it subject to planning permission. Planning was to be no longer merely a regulative function; 'Development Plans' were to be prepared for each area. In accordance with this wider conception of planning, powers were transferred from district councils to county councils, which were given greater powers of compulsory purchase, with coordination through the Ministry of Town and Country Planning. The act also gave the Board of Trade responsibility for securing a proper distribution of industry. This last provision had been anticipated in the 1945 Distribution of Industry Act, and some of the general planning developments had been initiated in a 1943 act. Nevertheless, the 1947 Town and Country Planning Act was an important measure in terms of attempting to control the environment, and a reflection of a growing trend among some in the party to concern themselves with environmental issues.

Other measures introduced in 1947 included an Agriculture Act, which continued on a permanent basis the wartime arrangements for guaranteed prices and markets. This helped raise farm income considerably, and generally encouraged the British agricultural sector, thus saving precious foreign currency; by 1950-1951 production had reached 146 per cent of the pre-war level.

1947 further saw the introduction of the long-delayed raising of the school-leaving age to 15. This had been accepted by the Cabinet in August 1945, though early 1947 saw an attempt by Dalton to persuade the Cabinet to reverse this decision to help alleviate the manpower gap. Educational arguments overcame Dalton's demands, but in general the government paid little attention to education, an omission which has frequently been criticised.[30] Certainly only a handful in the party had concerned themselves with education before the second world war, though there were notable exceptions, and many Labour supporters worked in organisations like the Workers' Educational Association. In 1945 there were great hopes about the 1944 Education Act. Ellen Wilkinson, the first Minister of Education, hoped to make the secondary modern school every bit as good as the grammar; the pursuit of equality was not necessarily seen as implying the treatment of different people in the same fashion. There was also a reluctance to undertake another major change quickly, particularly as the previous one had alienated some local, professional and religious interests. Pressures on building resources, government spending and time provided additional reasons for inaction. However, during 1945-1950 an increasing number in the party turned their attention to educational questions, and by 1951 the party was committed to the introduction of a comprehensive secondary system.[31]

After the passing of the second Reform Act in 1867, Robert Lowe, one of the Liberal leaders, proclaimed 'now we must educate our masters'. This was one Liberal lesson that the Labour Party adopted a little too slowly.

Chapter Six

THE AGE OF AUSTERITY, 1948-1950

'I know that many of you must be disappointed by continuing shortages and by the difficulties of getting enough clothes and household goods and that you feel impatient at having to listen to talks about economic problems or explanations of new Government White Papers.'

Sir Stafford Cripps in a radio broadcast on the 1948 Economic Survey, 10 March 1948. Text in Cripps Papers, 553/1080.

Part One: Economic Policy

As early as November 1945 the name of Cripps was being linked with austerity. 'Sir Austere Cripps' was the epithet coined by some Conservatives, though it was 1948 before the term austerity became a commonplace description of contemporary Britain. Subsequently the word was to give its name to the era: 'the age of austerity'.

Rationing was still widespread: coupons, or 'coupongs' as Cripps would say, were part of everyday life. It was accounted a triumph in a Cabinet paper that there would be 98 eggs per person in 1947-1948, compared to 87 in 1946-1947. However, in November 1948 Strachey told the cabinet that for the first time since 1944 it would be impossible to increase the meat ration in Christmas week.

In October 1947 the British public heard for the first time of snoek, an unfortunately named fish. The government had bought a large quantity from South Africa, and consignments began arriving in May 1948. In spite of ministerial tasting parties and the issuing of recipes like 'snoek piquante', this oily, tasteless fish proved less than popular. The government claimed to have sold all it bought, but rumour had it that the remnants had to be sold as cheap cat food in 1951.

A more serious problem was the so-called groundnuts scheme. In 1946 a Unilever subsidiary had approached the government with a plan to grow groundnuts in East Africa. This appealed particularly to the Minister of Food, who saw in the scheme a way of developing the area, saving foreign currency, producing a vital vegetable oil, and proving that state enterprise could work.[1] The result was a fiasco. Inadequate study had been made of the area; it proved difficult to clear (the need to use witch doctors to appease rain gods in the trees which were bulldozed down did not help − and prompted Conservative questions about which civil service pay scale these witch doctors were on!); and the nuts grew poorly. By 1949 the scheme was becoming a national issue, skillfully exploited by the Conservative press, which failed to point out that the idea originated with a private company, many of whose employees held important posts in the Ministry of Food.

During the late 1940s 'spivs' became a common term, referring to the amiable, if slightly unrespectable, characters who could obtain anything, at a price, off coupons; 'fell off a lorry' was a phrase which took on a new meaning. In late 1948 the Lynskey Tribunal investigated charges that civil servants, politicians and especially the Parliamentary Secretary at the Board of Trade had been receiving bribes from businessmen. The tribunal attracted considerable public attention, and revealed the shadier side of business in a Britain of shortages and controls; one businessman, when challenged by the Attorney General whether a phrase was a lie, answered 'It's not exactly a lie, it's a commercial term.' However, although virtually all civil servants and politicians were exonerated, the tribunal probably harmed Labour more than business: it helped confirm myths of the iniquities of controls, and the corruption that 'red tape' and 'bureaucracy' brought in their train.[2]

Physical controls were coming under increasing attack from the Conservatives and business by 1948, though some businessmen did well out of the controls; for example, price controls were fixed in agreement with an industry, often at relatively high levels. Many consumers also clearly resented some controls, such as the Utility Scheme, which set standards for some goods, but limited choice − though again these schemes were often advantageous to consumers. In 1948 Professor J. Jewkes published a book entitled *Ordeal by Planning* which summed up many of the criticisms, and included examples of planning in action: of the despatch of a small shipment of lubricating oil involving filling in forty-six forms; of a provincial corn merchant who operated under fourteen licences and with one hundred and sixty fixed prices; of a company fined for selling 60,000 frying pans on the home market because of delays in the Board of Trade supplying an export licence; and so on. The book did not detail the problem which would have occurred in a post-war Britain without controls, and many subsequent critics have failed to discuss what would have happened had the free market reigned supreme, as it had done after the first world war.[3]

However, these criticisms struck a note which was echoed, in more moderate form, by many in the Labour government which was increasingly turning away from controls as a form of economic regulation. Beer has seen this development in terms of the problems which emerged concerning physical planning, opposition from business, or the unions.[4] Unquestionably these factors had some influence. Nevertheless, it is important to realise that from the outset many in the Cabinet saw most controls as temporary measures: at the Cabinet meeting on 16 August 1945 the Home Secretary had reported that the coalition Supplies and Services (Transitional Powers) Bill only gave powers to continue wartime regulations for two years; this was considered inadequate to cover the 'transition', but its duration was only extended to five years.

During 1948 there was a gradual relaxation of controls, and in November, Harold Wilson, who had succeeded Cripps as President of the Board of Trade in 1947, announced a 'bonfire' of controls on Guy Fawkes day. This removed a variety of restrictions which had previously required the issue of 200,000 licences a year. During 1949-1950 there was a further gradual relaxation of controls.

Cooperation with industry rather than control was increasingly becoming the order of the day. Already in 1947 Cripps had passed an Industrial Organization and Development Act, which gave the government powers to set up in certain industries Development Councils, including industrialists, trade unionists and independent members to advise on efficiency, collect statistics and perform other functions of mutual use. Wilson strenuously sought to set up such councils, though with only limited success. The Federation of British Industry and companies were showing growing concern about the talk of further nationalisation, and on the other hand were hopeful of the imminent return of a Conservative government: Labour was entering a 'lame duck' period to some extent. The 1948 Monopolies Act also did not involve a serious interference with industry. *Let Us Face the Future* had promised to supervise monopolies and cartels, but Labour in effect encouraged them where concentration seemed efficient, and there was no concerted effort to end restrictive practices. The 1948 act simply set up a Monopolies and Restrictive Practices Commission with powers to inquire and recommend action, but no more. It was clearly designed to encourage cooperation with the government over pricing and other policies, rather than to exert direct control over industry.[5]

The government also sought to obtain cooperation with the management and especially unions over wages policy. This issue had first been raised in the Cabinet on 14 March 1946, when there had been a sharp clash between Morrison and Bevin. Many saw a clear contradiction in attempting to plan an economy where wages were settled independently of the government, but the unions were hostile to interference in this sphere, and jealously guarded differentials. However, it was general inflationary pressure rather than a desire to influence differentials which led the government in January 1947 to issue a statement, endorsed by the National Joint Advisory Council, which drew attention to the need to keep incomes and prices down in order to remain competitive in world markets. With full employment, wages were showing a marked tendency to rise, though union moderation and a system of compulsory arbitration helped keep down the number of strikes: during 1945-1951 only 14,260,000 man days were lost through strikes, compared to 192,230,000 in the seven years after the first world war.[6]

In February 1948 the government issued another document, entitled *Statement on Personal Incomes, Costs and Prices*. This sought a total standstill on profits and rents, and a limitation of wage increases. The government was well enough aware of union support for free collective bargaining not to interfere directly, but it drew attention to its statement in Wages Councils and other negotiating bodies. The policy was endorsed by the TUC, and a conference of trade union executives in March 1948 did likewise, though with some reservations. It was clear that loyalty to the government was a major factor, for behind the scenes there was a strong opposition to the policy. Wage restraint lasted until 1950, when rising prices, and hostility within the unions to any form of pay policy, led to its breakdown.

The 1948 Economic Survey, issued in March, further sought to tackle the problem of rising wages by seeking to increase unemployment 50 per cent, especially by cutting the building programme. There was a growing belief among economists that Britain had over-full employment.[7] Beveridge had talked of full employment as leaving 3 per cent unemployed: Britain's average in 1948 was 1.8 per cent. Andrew Shonfield has described the statement in the 1948 Survey as courageous,[8] but the government did little to increase significantly unemployment. Indeed, in 1949 the average was 1.6 per cent, and in 1950 it was 1.5 per cent. Nothing short of a considerable increase would have been likely to ease inflationary pressure; such a policy would have been strongly opposed by the unions and by the less technocratic members of the party, who would have seen it as barbarous rather than brave.

The 1948 Economic Survey was in general more precise and detailed than its 1947 counterpart, but there were clear signs of a declining faith in this form of planning. Its proposals were described as only a 'tentative Budget', and some of the failings of the 1947 Survey were noted. In the autumn of 1948 Labour published a 'Long Term Programme' to illustrate how the country could achieve economic independence by 1952, but this was more or less a condition of Marshall aid, which began to flow into Britain on a large scale in 1948. Although the government continued to publish the Economic Survey until 1951, by 1950 it was a 'humble document, meek almost to the point of being meaningless' in the words of the *Economist* on 1 April 1950.

Budgetary policy was now becoming increasingly important, a reflection of Cripps's and general Labour views about Keynesianism, more than those of the Treasury, or problems with planning, as some have implied.[9] Cripps's budgets were deflationary. In 1948 he budgeted for a surplus of £300 million, though an American recession led to a lower surplus estimate in 1949. The main innovation of the 1948 budget was a Special Contribution, which levied a once-and-for-all tax on investment income over £250 per annum. The main theme was the need to increase exports; Cripps in the budget speech argued that Marshall aid gave only limited time in which to improve Britain's export performance. 1949 saw further attempts to stimulate industrial investment; a 40 per cent tax remission was given on profits ploughed back into new plant, and the tax on distributed profits was raised to 30 per cent. At the same time, there was an effort to limit government spending. A ceiling was put on food subsidies; in 1948 they had cost £485 million, but a limit of £465 million was imposed for 1949. A ceiling was also imposed on social service expenditure, which with the introduction of the NHS and other benefits in 1948 was rising rapidly. Health and insurance expenditure in 1946 stood at £334 million, but by 1948 the figure was £598 million, and in 1950 it was £835 million. In October 1949 Cripps wanted to make cuts in public expenditure of £700 million, but this met with strong opposition, notably from Bevan, who threatened to resign if there were major cuts in social service spending.[10] The Cabinet on 21 October agreed to cuts totalling £250 million, but deep divisions remained over the ever-mounting cost of the social services.

These further cuts in October 1949 followed the devaluation of the pound in September. The balance of payments situation had improved dramatically since 1946-1947. From deficits of £230 million in 1946 and £381 million in 1947, Britain moved to a surplus of £26 million in 1948 and a deficit of £1 million in 1949. Exports showed a remarkable rise, 77 per cent during 1946-1950, and 25 per cent during 1947-1948 alone — a remarkable success for indicative planning. However, currency was leaving Britain at a rapid rate. Dalton had told the first Cabinet on 7 August that specific exchange control laws would not be required as control could be achieved under the Supplies and Services (Transitional Powers) Act, but subsequent Labour efforts in this field were less than successful. Between 1947 and 1949 £645 million in private capital left Britain. It is difficult to break this sum down, but probably only half was genuine investment. The government faced a general problem over the export of capital by undervaluing exports, overvaluing imports, and other devices to evade exchange controls, which was especially easy because of weaker controls in other sterling area countries. Improvements in exports therefore were to some extent counteracted by capital outflows, and reserves remained relatively small. The problem for the pound was made worse in 1949 by a mild recession in the USA, which helped lead to a dollar deficit in the second quarter of 1949 far larger than had been anticipated in the Economic Survey. Other sterling countries were also running up large dollar deficits. Against this background, there was renewed speculation against the pound, encouraged by clear American support for devaluation.[11]

On 15 June the Cabinet was told that the American government expected a prolonged recession, and its main desires had reverted to convertibility and non-discrimination, rather than helping Europe, or combating communism. Before the Cabinet meeting on 1 July, Cripps was told by the American Secretary of State that British export prices were not competitive. However, Cripps and many of his advisers were opposed to devaluation, supporting instead cuts in food subsidies and general deflation. There was some prejudice against devaluation on the grounds that it might be seen as symbolising Britain's failure. More seriously, there were arguments that it would import inflation, while not increasing exports greatly because of continued production difficulties. The Cabinet therefore rejected devaluation.

Shortly afterwards Cripps left for Switzerland to convalesce after an illness. Economic policy was taken over by a group of ministers, including Attlee, Wilson, Hugh Gaitskell, the rising Minister of Fuel and Power, and Douglas Jay, the Economic Secretary at the Treasury. As the situation worsened, with increasing speculation similar to 1931,[12] Gaitskell and Jay became convinced of the need to devalue; Wilson and Attlee came round to this point of view as well. There was some opposition from officials, who when overruled wanted devaluation to be accompanied by convertibility and expenditure cuts, mainly to impress American opinion. However, by the beginning of August it had been decided to devalue without introducing convertibility. This was presented to Cripps, and subsequently to the Cabinet, as a *fait accompli*.

On 18 September 1949 a devaluation of 30 per cent was announced, from $4.03 to $2.80 to the pound. Many have subsequently argued that the figure was too high in the light of prices and elasticities, that 20 per cent might have been a more sensible figure.[13] The figure of 30 per cent seems to have been mainly political, to impress the Americans. Since the introduction of Marshall aid the Americans had appointed what ammounted virtually to an overseer of the British economy, and the government was keen not to have to make large cuts in public spending, or introduce convertibility, both of which were thought desirable in some American circles. Nevertheless, the 30 per cent figure was to help in fuelling inflation, with serious effects on the government's popularity in 1950-1951.

Part Two: Foreign, Defence and Colonial Policy

During 1948-1950 external affairs continued to pose major problems for the government, though to some extent foreign policy became a less divisive issue in the Labour Party. The cold war which had been developing during 1945-1947 became an obvious reality during 1948-1950 (a development symbolised by the creation in January 1948 of a secret Foreign Office department to supply, both externally and internally, anti-communist propaganda). Whatever the rights and wrongs of this development, it became more difficult to argue the case for pursuing friendly relations with the Soviet Union. At the same time, more conservative governments emerged in leading western European countries, making the 'Third Force' case more problematic (though it could have been argued that the cold war helped these conservative victories), and adding weight to those in the party who opposed European unity.

The development of the cold war and emergence of conservative governments can be seen clearly in the case of Germany. During 1947 and 1948 troubles with the Soviet Union, economic needs, and American pressure had led to further unity among the western zones. In 1948 this was accompanied by moves to establish a west German state. The cold war, plus the success of the re-education programme and Allied attempts to revive German political life, made such a development possible. This meant the dropping of the plan to nationalise certain German industries, which the Labour government had sought since 1945, but the structure of the new state was a federal one – a conception which fitted in well with Labour's earlier desire to prevent the re-emergence of a strong central government.

Against this background, the Soviet Union decided to institute a land blockade of Berlin. Berlin was 100 miles inside the Soviet zone, but was governed by the four powers in a microcosm of the German situation. On 24 June the Cabinet was told that the blockade had begun in earnest. The pretext was the introduction of a currency reform already implemented in the western zones. Behind this probably lay a dual desire either to force the western powers back to the negotiating table on terms more favourable to Russia, or simply to drive them out of the old German capital.

In the British Cabinet Bevan supported relieving Berlin by tank thrust, a surprising line from someone who had earlier shown sympathy for the Soviet Union's position, and indicative of how opinions had changed.[14] Certainly there was a strong fear about general Soviet intentions: agreement was hastily reached with the Americans permitting them to station atomic bombers on British soil, and to fly missions against the USSR should war break out. However, Attlee and Bevin were anxious to avoid provocation; Bevin pressed the USA not to take the issue to the UN because it might seem provocative, and to preclude bilateral negotiations. They had no intention of withdrawing in the face of threats, a decision strongly supported by most people in Britain. Gallup in October 1948 found that 64 per cent wanted Britain to stay in Berlin, and only 18 per cent wanted a withdrawal. Therefore a massive Anglo-American airlift was organised to the beleaguered city. The Soviet Union did not stop this airlift, fearing that it would lead to an escalation, and by May 1949 the blockade had been lifted.

In the very same month a Basic Law was proclaimed in West Germany, setting up a federal German state. By the end of 1949 elections had been held in the west, resulting in a Christian Democrat victory. Earlier in 1949 an eastern German Democratic Republic had been established – a Germany in which, as Bevin told the Cabinet in 1948, political opponents of the USSR were held in former Nazi concentration camps![15]

While Germany was dividing into two, other moves were taking place to promote greater unity within western Europe. Though these developments were often associated with the cold war itself, they were also related to more purely economic or supranational motives.

The idea of European unity was an old one, and some moves towards this end preceded even the end of the second world war. However, the first major post-war organisation was the Organisation for European Economic Cooperation. The purpose of the OEEC was to administer Marshall aid. As such, it was fully supported by the British government. However, its essentially economic and functionalist aspect did not satisfy some of the European supranationalists, and in May 1948 an unofficial conference was called at the Hague to discuss further unity.

Labour's response was cautious, even hostile. Labour had an internationalist tradition in official policy statements, and people like Attlee and Bevin had made references even before the second world war to the need for greater European cooperation, especially economic. After the war, many had considered the left-wing, or partially left, governments in countries like France and Italy an added reason for considering European cooperation, particularly in a world which appeared to be dividing into two camps.

During 1948 there began a clear right-wing trend in elections across Europe. At the same time, there were growing fears about the loss of control over the British economy, in particular the newly nationalised industries. Historically, Britain had sought a free hand in Europe, a policy fitting an imperial power. For all Labour's internationalist claims, there were many in the party who held strong nationalist views, who looked to the Commonwealth as the natural sphere of British cooperation. Furthermore, there were many who did not fully realise how much Britain's world position had declined. Others who perceived this transition sought cooperation with the United States rather than a prostrate Europe; the policies were seen as incompatible in that a united Europe might encourage American isolationism.

In January 1948 Bevin made his famous 'Western Union' speech in the House of Commons, hailed by some as the most momentous speech he ever made on foreign policy.[16] In reality, its call for a united Europe was vague. Subsequently Bevin strongly opposed a French proposal which emerged from the Hague congress proposing political and economic union expressed through a Consultative Assembly drawn from the parliaments of the member states. In September 1948 he told the House of Commons that one could not build the roof before the building itself, that there was need for cooperation in more limited fields first. In November 1948

Bevin asked Dalton, a well known anti-federalist, to lead the British delegation at a conference in Paris to consider the next steps which should be taken towards closer union in Europe. The result was the Council of Europe, set up in May 1949. The Council very much represented a victory for the British point of view, being essentially functionalist, with power remaining in the hands of the member governments. It was a great disappointment to those who sought a more supranational body; many in Europe began to plan for a united Europe without Britain.

Britain was far keener on European cooperation in the limited, though important, field of defence. In March 1947 Britain had signed a fifty-year treaty with France, and in 1948 this had been broadened to include the Benelux countries in the Treaty of Brussels. On the day of the signing of this treaty, in a speech to Congress, Truman had spoken of American willingness to help the 'free countries' of Europe defend themselves. This encouraged the Brussels Treaty powers, led by Bevin, who had been working towards securing a formal American commitment, to explore the possibility of an agreement with the USA. The result was the signing in April 1949 of the North Atlantic Treaty Organisation convention, according to Francis Williams 'one of the great moments in Bevin's life'.[17]

NATO ran into some criticism from the Labour left, which claimed that it would further divide the world, and that it was incompatible with collective security. In the House of Commons in May 1949 Philip Noel-Baker, the Minister of Commonwealth Relations, described the pact as only a stop-gap until a real collective pact could be achieved. Bevin claimed that the pact was defensive, it was simply to deter aggression. He further claimed that NATO was consistent with the UN Charter. Parties to the pact were committed to end their disputes peacefully, and there was strong emphasis on international cooperation for economic stability. It was an excellent example of Labour's realism tinged with idealism, though the provisions of the pact cannot be attributed simply to British desires.

In spite of membership of NATO, British defence spending remained relatively high, a reflection of international tensions. In 1948 Britain spent more than the other Brussels Treaty powers put together, and proportionately more than the USA.[18] The government was trying to cut expenditure. During the winter of 1947-1948 it imposed a ceiling of £600 million on defence spending for 1949-1950, whereas the Chiefs of Staff wanted £825 million. The number of men in the armed forces was being run down, dropping from over 1 million in 1947, to 940,000 in 1948, 800,000 in 1949, and 750,000 in 1950. Overseas expenditure on the forces was being cut, from £200 million in 1947 to £113 million in

1948 and £98 million in 1949. However, in September 1948 Morrison told the House of Commons that there was a need for increased spending in 1950. Technological change, for example in jet aircraft production, was requiring large expenditure; more importantly, external developments and pressures militated against further cuts.

The beginning of communist guerilla activity in Malaya further added to British expenses on the colonial front. In spite of the British withdrawal from India in 1947, and Ceylon and Burma in 1948, Britain remained committed to parts of south east Asia, and elsewhere. British policy continued to reflect mixed motives. Some have argued that after the economic crisis of 1947 Britain became increasingly parasitic on her colonies.[19] The truth is more complex. In his Western Union speech Bevin talked of pooling colonial resources, and at other times he seemed keen to use these assets to maintain British power and living standards. But there were other attempts to help colonies. Certainly the Colonial Office tried hard to defend colonial interests. Often these aspects overlapped, as in the groundnuts scheme, which Gupta has misleadingly described as showing Strachey's 'imperial bias'.[20] In some ways this period saw a decline in emphasis on colonial and Commonwealth cooperation, especially as growing divisions emerged politically. Certainly by the time of the Colombo conference in 1950 Bevin was showing little interest in any serious form of economic cooperation.

Part Three: Legislation and Reform

Although the Labour government during 1948-1950 was continually plagued by the economic crisis and deteriorating international situation, it did not neglect domestic reform.

1948 saw, after a long struggle, the implementation of the 1946 National Health Service Act. The bill had received the Royal Assent in November 1946, but opposition from the BMA had continued unabated; indeed, if anything its hysteria increased.[21]

In December 1946, acting on a mandate from a referendum of members which showed that 54 per cent were opposed to cooperation with the new scheme, the BMA leaders refused to discuss with Bevan conditions of service. An impasse seemed to have been reached. However, in early January the heads of the Royal Colleges wrote to Bevan in a spirit of compromise, requesting clarifications about promises on the questions of not introducing a salaried service, the right of appeal against dismissal, and freedom of movement of general practitioners, together with the right of specialists to continue private practice. Bevan replied in a conciliatory fashion. The BMA was suspicious of the motives of the specialists, who seemed set to do well out of the NHS (and who had little interest in the BMA's concern over the sale of practices), but decided to reopen negotiations. These continued until December 1947 when a new crisis took place.

A further referendum was held, and the doctors voted this time by nine to one against service under the act. In February the government staged a major debate in the House of Commons, welcoming the introduction of the service on 5 July. Bevan made a rousing speech, and the debate was well publicised, but it is doubtful whether, as Michael Foot has claimed, this was crucial in changing the attitude of the BMA.[22] More important was a new initiative from the Royal College of Physicians, a reflection of Bevan's belief in behind-the-scenes manoeuvring rather than Bagehotian Parliamentary education. Bevan had reopened his lines of communication with Lord Moran, 'Corkscrew Charlie' as he was known to those who had witnessed his machinations. Moran persuaded the Royal College of Physicians to pass a resolution calling upon Bevan to amend the act so as to make it impossible to introduce a full-time salaried staff without passing a new act. Bevan immediately agreed, and called for further talks with the BMA.

The BMA remained suspicious of the specialists, and the die-hards were out for blood. However, the doctors did not have public opinion on their side. Gallup found that 69 per cent thought the NHS a good thing, while only 13 per cent were opposed. Some, especially the younger doctors, welcomed the scheme; others who received a significant part of their income from the old Lloyd George system needed to sign up to make good the financial loss they would suffer when the old system ended. By April 1948 twenty per cent of the doctors had joined the NHS, not hordes but enough to worry the BMA that its army might be near to desertion. The BMA was divided, and ordered another referendum, adding the condition that at least 13,000 GPs would have to vote against participation if the BMA was to maintain an effective opposition. The result was that only 9,588 did (17,037 had voted against in the previous referendum). The BMA Council and Representative Body, after long and bitter meetings, decided to give way.

Bevan's sense of bitterness against the BMA, and the support the doctors had received from the Conservatives, bubbled to the surface in a speech which he made at Belle Vue on 4 July 1948, the eve of the introduction of the NHS. In this speech he referred to Conservatives as 'lower than vermin'. Bevan later claimed that this was taken out of context, that he was not referring to all Conservatives; but in the enthusiasm of the night this was not what he said. The gaffe was a godsend to the Conservatives' speech writers. Conservative MPs claimed that Bevan was their best propagandist; Laski, hardly a man of verbal discretion, considered the speech lost Labour two million votes in the next election. This was undoubtedly a gross exaggeration, but Bevan, the great latter-day Labour mythologist, had provided a superb godsend to Conservative mythologists who sought to portray Labour as socially divisive.

The emotion revealed at Belle Vue in retrospect seems even more misguided. Within a year the vast majority of doctors had happily joined the scheme, and large numbers of patients were receiving free treatment. For example, in the first year 5,250,000 pairs of spectacles were dispensed, in part a reflection of pent-up demand. No longer did the poor have to test their own eyes at Woolworths. The NHS provided free care for all who needed it. However, total opthalmic expenditure in the first year was £22 million, compared to a 1944 estimate of £1 million, and the NHS in general was quickly to make financial demands vastly in excess of anything envisaged by its creators. This was to pose a growing problem for Labour during 1948-1951.

The NHS was a major reform. It had been created in the face of considerable opposition from the doctors, and there seems no doubt that a Conservative government would have introduced a distinctly less ambitious scheme. Even so, it is important not to overstate the radicalism of the reform, or excessively praise Bevan's 'heroic struggle', as many have done.[23] He almost certainly contributed to his own difficulties by shunning the BMA in the early stages of planning the service; he never seriously attempted to use public opinion against the doctors. Partly because of this, he felt it necessary to make concessions to the specialists that allowed the continuation of a private medicine system, which critics at the time pointed out was likely to lead to dual standards, as well as being morally wrong. If Bevan truly trusted the people rather than manoeuvring, the NHS might have been more genuinely an equal service.

The 1948 National Assistance Act similarly completed work begun in 1945-1946, in this case complementing the National Insurance Act. The 1948 act ended the Poor Law, which had its origins in Elizabethan times. It acted as a safety net, providing payments for all who did not qualify for insurance benefits. It further required local authorities to provide residential accommodation for persons who, by reason of age, infirmity, or other hardship, required attention not otherwise available, and to provide temporary accomodation in emergencies, though not all local authorities were adequately to satisfy these conditions. National Assistance payments were also means-tested, which angered many, and the scheme was not integrated into a single social security system; recipients of National Assistance were therefore encouraged to feel different, even inferior.

The 1949 Housing Act sought to improve the local authorities' performance in building and improving houses. Housing during 1948-1950 was still an issue which plagued Labour. Bevan's housing programme was producing fewer homes than initially planned, especially after cutbacks in 1947-1948 as a result of the economic crisis. In 1946 new building had provided 55,811 homes, with just over half coming from the private sector; by 1948 this had risen to 227,938, with over 80 per cent coming from the public sector; but in 1949 and 1950 building fell to just under 20,000 homes in each year. By June 1948 eight sites for new towns had been approved, but progress was slow, particularly after legal wrangles over Stevenage; by the end of 1950 only 451 houses had been completed. In the 1951 census it was estimated that there were 728,420 more households than homes, though the real discrepancy was probably more like 1,400,000. Housing was naturally an area in which the government's record was seen as less than impressive; Gallup in January 1949 found that only 29 per cent were satisfied with the government's record, compared to 61 per cent who were not. There was especially strong discontent among the working class, the very people whom Bevan tried to help; additionally, there was some discontent among mainly middle-class prospective owner-occupiers. The 1949 Housing Act significantly increased Exchequer subsidies, but in the short run it had little effect on the housing shortage. The 1949 Landlord and Tenant Rent Control Act, which gave tribunal powers to fix rents in unfurnished tenancies, was similarly a useful act, but one which did little in the short run to assuage discontent.

Other reforms dealing with 'social justice' and the quality of life were passed. The 1948 Children Act instructed local authorities to set up children committees with professional child officers to concern themselves with establishing a secure family environment for children in care. The 1948 Criminal Justice Act abolished corporal punishment (the Lords deleted a clause in the bill abolishing hanging — a decision which most in the Cabinet supported). The 1949 Legal Aid and Advice Act provided legal help for the poor. The 1948 Employment and Training Act created the first comprehensive youth employment scheme. And the 1949 National Park and Access to the Countryside Act represented a somewhat belated government attempt to preserve Britain's beauty.

Many of these reforms, and earlier ones, affected the position of local government, yet local government was an area to which Labour devoted little time. In 1943 a Labour statement entitled *The Future of Local Government* had argued the need for larger units to provide services more efficiently, though recognising the democratic aspects of small units. In fact, Labour thinking was moving more and more towards strong central control. Some of the early Fabians, especially the Webbs, had supported the municipalisation of many industries and services; they thought that local government could be both an efficient provider of certain services, notably gas and water, and remain sensitive to local needs to fulfil a democratic purpose by bringing government closer to the people. These views had never appealed to the more collective and nationally orientated majority of union leaders, and Labour intellectuals too had grown to see the advantages of central government in ensuring uniformity in the provision of services, and even controlling non-Labour areas, though again this was not an area which had attracted much attention, and there was far from uniformity of opinion.

During 1945-1950 Labour's reforms removed many powers from local authorities, for example in the field of health, though they added new ones in housing and elsewhere. These changes were not accompanied by a major reform of local government, in part a reflection of Labour's lack of interest, though shortage of Parliamentary time, and the opposition of existing local authorities to change, were also important. Nevertheless, in 1948 Parliament passed a local government act which introduced several useful changes. One provision of the act was to allow the payment of expenses to councillors, an attempt to widen the social basis of councils. Another clause allowed councils to levy a rate for cultural activities. The most important aspect was the introduction of a new grant known as the Exchequer Equalisation grant. The principle behind this was that the Exchequer became liable to make up any deficiency between an authority's rateable value per head, and the average for the whole country. The purpose was to help the poorer areas, whose needs might be great, but rateable value low. At the same time, the Inland Revenue took over responsibility for assessing rateable values; previously local authorities had not been entirely consistent in assessing values.[24]

Labour's nationalisation of gas in 1948 clearly indicates the lack of support for municipalisation, other than among the local authorities themselves, who owned 36 per cent of capacity in 1945. The 1945 Heyworth Report on the gas industry had recommended nationalisation, and this was already the policy of the government. Gas production and supply were organised regionally, though with a national Gas Council to control certain aspects of the industry. Again, this was a relatively uncontroversial measure, though some Conservatives put up a strong filibuster in committee, and the bill received the Royal Assent in July 1948.[25]

The nationalisation of iron and steel was to be a very different story. It was by far the most controversial of Labour's measures, though it is misleading to claim that it entailed 'a serious threat to the "private sector" ', as Miliband has done.[26] Even so, the bill was strongly opposed by the industry and the Conservatives.[27]

The iron and steel industry in the inter-war years had been in a state of depression, until the imposition of a tariff, together with general world recovery and rearmament in the 1930s, had led to a boom. Protection had been linked with a demand for reorganisation, and in May 1945 the coalition government had asked the Iron and Steel Federation to produce a five-year plan for reorganisation to make the industry more efficient. The steel owners agreed, and accepted that government aid would be required, though rejecting nationalisation.

Support for nationalisation had developed in the main union in the industry during the depression, but was dropped from the 1937 Labour *Immediate Programme*. Pressure from the floor at the 1944 Labour conference, and TUC support, led to its inclusion in *Let Us Face the Future*. However, some in the party leadership remained less than enthusiastic about the measure. It was partly because of this that the bill was delayed so long, though problems with drafting and Parliamentary time would have made it difficult to take in the first session.

John Wilmot, the Minister of Supply, was responsible for the iron and steel industry. In November 1945 he circulated a memorandum advocating nationalisation, though he suggested waiting until the Iron and Steel Federation had published its reorganisation scheme. This was agreed by the Cabinet.[28] The report came out in December, and within the Ministry of Supply there was a feeling that it represented a workable scheme for reorganisation. Wilmot disagreed, and in February 1946 he decided to proceed with nationalisation for three main reasons: first, the industry was a quasi-monopoly; secondly, it was of great importance to other industries and its production targets were somewhat modest; and thirdly, the government would have to find much of the reorganisation finance anyway. Furthermore, it was not clear that the Iron and Steel Federation had the support of the whole industry for the implementation of the plan.

In spite of these arguments, there remained opposition to the measure in the government. Morrison in particular feared that it might hinder production at a critical time, though he accepted that its inclusion in the 1945 manifesto meant that Labour was under some obligation to proceed.[29] Eventually, in April the Cabinet decided to go ahead with nationalisation, but in the 1947-1948 session, rather than accept Wilmot's proposal for 1946-1947. The Cabinet decided that in the interim period the industry would be run by a Control Board, with a brief to collect information and generally to prepare for nationalisation. The industry was a complex one, with large amounts of vertical and horizontal integration. The hostility of the steel owners to nationalisation tended to reinforce the problem, as the government did not have detailed knowledge of all aspects of the industry. Predictably, the Iron and Steel Federation refused to cooperate with the Control Board, and in August the Cabinet decided to remove the requirement for the Board to prepare for nationalisation. As a result, the steel industry agreed to participate in the Board.

In March 1947 the ministry produced a scheme to take over the 'heavy core' of the industry, comprising basically the manufacture of iron ore, pig iron, steel and rerolled products – involving one hundred and five companies. There had been considerable discussion about the form of compensation, but by this time Wilmot favoured the stock market valuation system, the format used in the transport, electricity and gas bills. This scheme was discussed during the spring of 1947 in various committees and the Cabinet itself. The question again proved divisive, especially as it became tied up with whether to take gas first, and the need for a new Parliament Act. Finally, in May 1947 the Cabinet reaffirmed its decision to proceed with nationalisation in the 1947-1948 session.

The industry objected, and an approach was made to Attlee, Morrison and Wilmot over the question of a compromise. The representatives of the steel industry argued that nationalisation would dislocate the industry, that there would be no unified control, and the proposed scheme left out some parts of the industry in need of aid. Attlee agreed that Morrison and Wilmot should investigate the possibility of a compromise. Attlee was thought at the time to be equivocal, even opposed to nationalisation. Certainly he had no strong views on the issue. Nevertheless, there are some reasons to think that his actions were designed to discredit Morrison, even possibly Bevin, who was growing more equivocal over the issue, especially as the leadership of the main steel union was becoming less interested in nationalisation and attracted by promises of profit sharing. This was a time of mounting plots against Attlee's leadership, and he lacked nothing in guile, though it is important not always to read Machiavellian motives into his actions.

Morrison and Wilmot duly arrived at a compromise, and this was put to the Cabinet in July. It involved public supervision of the industry, and the acceptance of nationalisation of parts of the industry, on the recommendation of the Control Board, where there was proven to be inefficiency. This compromise was strongly opposed by most in the Cabinet, notably Cripps and Bevan, who threatened to resign.[30] Attlee, who had remained virtually silent throughout, therefore concluded that the suggestion was unacceptable.

The Cabinet decided to consult the trade unions concerned. On 1 August a meeting was arranged with representatives from the TUC; time was requested to ascertain opinion. Before the TUC replied the Cabinet met again on 7 August and decided to accept nationalisation. The supporters of nationalisation within the Cabinet were pushing the measure strongly. Backbench pressures for nationalisation were mounting. And although there was growing discontent in the party over the nature of nationalisation, especially the absence of worker participation (this was to cause a heated discussion at the 1948 Labour conference), there was clearly considerable support for iron and steel nationalisation. However, the Cabinet decided that the introduction of the measure in the 1947-1948 session might have to be reconsidered if the economic situation continued to worsen. On 14 October the Cabinet agreed to delay the measure until the 1948-1949 session.

Earlier in October Wilmot had been replaced as Minister of Supply, a victim of the attempt to produce a compromise. Bevan was offered the post, but he was in the middle of his troubles with the BMA, so he refused. The new minister was G.R. Strauss, who had been Parliamentary Secretary at the Ministry of Transport. He therefore had experience of the nationalisation programme; he was also a wealthy man involved in the metal-broking trade, and had some knowledge of the iron and steel industry.

In March 1948 Strauss circulated a printed draft of the bill. In an accompanying memorandum he pointed out that iron and steel was a more complex industry than any nationalised before, and that the present nationalisation scheme might impose too heavy a burden on the proposed corporation. He therefore advocated two less ambitious alternatives. After some discussion, the Cabinet on 14 June 1948 decided to accept the median proposal, and to proceed in the 1948-1949 session. Support for the measure in the party was now too great to back down.

The bill was published in October 1948. It ran into strong Conservative opposition in the House of Commons, and was easily the hardest-fought of the nationalisation bills. At the outset the Conservatives attempted to have this bill declared hybrid; this was rejected by the Speaker (Parliamentary Counsel had paid considerable attention to this question). Subsequently bitter struggles ensued on the floor of the House of Commons, and in committee; together with transport, it was the only nationalisation bill which needed to be passed with the guillotine. The Conservatives claimed that the bill was about power, rather than efficiency or need. They argued that it was simply a way of creating 'jobs for the boys'; the compensation terms were attacked as inadequate. There was little justification for these charges; most Conservative opposition was more a ritualistic self-assertion than academic critique. Gallup polls showed that the measure was unpopular; in November 1948 only 24 per cent supported iron and steel nationalisation, while 44 per cent were opposed. The Conservatives generally were doing well, in opinion polls, though it is wrong to imply, as some have done, that this was a reflection of their growing opposition in Parliament.[31] If anything, the causality ran in the opposite direction; Parliamentary politics were not that important to the electorate.

However, Labour retained a large majority in the House of Commons, and the bill was passed substantially unchanged. In the Lords the bill ran into the predicted troubles. The Lords in particular attempted to amend the vesting date to 1 July 1951, after the next general election. Initially, it seemed that the government might be forced to invoke the Parliament Act, but this would still have delayed the vesting date until after the election. In November 1949 it was therefore announced that the vesting date would not be earlier than 1 January 1951, and the Lords passed the bill. It received the Royal Assent on 24 November 1949.

Iron and steel was Labour's last nationalisation measure. When it came into effect in 1951 2,306,900 people were employed in nationalised industries, ten per cent of the working population. However, in general these industries were more a liability than an asset to the government. Some, like coal, were semi-derelict, industries which would have posed massive problems for anyone. Some, like electricity, were natural monopolies; this, and the fact that they were 'public service' industries, constituted good reason for nationalising them, but it also meant that price rises would be blamed on the government, even if prices were often below the market rate, thus depressing profits, and opening a further line of attack. Iron and steel did not mean that Labour took charge of the commanding heights of the economy, nor even that it took over a truly profitable industry, for its pre-nationalisation profits stemmed from special circumstances. Overall, nationalisation was piecemeal, lacking a serious gradualist strategy, owing more to union pressures than reason. It was a heritage that was to plague Labour in years to come.

There was a certain irony in the government agreeing to the House of Lords' desire to delay the iron and steel vesting date. The government had introduced at the beginning of the 1947-1948 session a new Parliament Bill to reduce the powers of the Lords' veto under the 1911 act from three sessions over a minimum of two years, to two sessions over a minimum of a year. This bill was in part introduced because of anticipated opposition from the Lords over iron and steel nationalisation. Although Miliband has criticised the role of the Lords at this time,[32] up until the iron and steel bill the government had run into no serious problems with the Lords, who followed the so-called Salisbury doctrine of not opposing measures included in the 1945 Labour manifesto. Indeed, the Lords had acted as a quite useful second chamber for detailed criticisms of parts of bills that had not received adequate attention in a hurried Commons. In 1946, for example, the Lords passed 1,222 amendments to government bills, and all but 57 were accepted. This is not to defend the Lords as an institution; the point is simply that it did not mutilate Labour legislation, or even significantly alter it, in the way the Lords had done during previous radical governments.

Although *Let Us Face the Future* had stated that 'we give clear notice that we will not tolerate obstruction of the people's will by the House of Lords', the Lords did not consider this a specific commitment to a new Parliament Bill; it was also argued that people did not support a new bill, a claim which opinion polls supported: in November 1947 Gallup found that 45 per cent wanted the Lords left alone, while 32 per cent wanted its powers decreased, and 5 per cent wanted them increased. During February-April 1948 discussions took place between all parties on the question of Lords' reform, but no agreement could be reached on delaying powers, though agreement was achieved over the introduction of paid life peers and women members. The Lords rejected the Parliament Bill in June; it was passed again in an extraordinary session in September 1948, and, under the 1911 act, received the Royal Assent on 16 December 1949 – the last major act passed by the 1945-1950 Labour government.[33]

Previously Labour had passed three other constitutional acts. The Ireland Act of 1949 resulted from the termination by the southern Irish government of its limited association with the British Commonwealth. The 1949 act stated that Northern Ireland would remain part of the

United Kingdom until its own parliament voted otherwise, a provision which led sixty-three Labour MPs to vote against the government; the British presence in Ireland for some was an imperial rather than domestic matter. Far less controversial were the 1948 and 1949 Representation of the People Acts. These introduced a major redistribution and changes in electoral law. Plural voting was abolished; university constituencies were therefore ended; and two-member constituencies were broken up. The Home Secretary, Chuter Ede, claimed that these measures completed the 'progress of the British people towards a full and complete democracy, begun by the great Reform Bill of 1832'.[34] Whilst in no way comparing with the great reform bills of 1832, 1867, 1883-1884 and 1918, these changes undoubtedly made the system more democratic.

It was under this new system that Britain went to the polls in 1950 to cast judgement on the 1945-1950 Labour government.

Chapter Seven

THE 1950 GENERAL ELECTION

> *'you must expect the new programme to be of a somewhat different character and a somewhat different tempo from the last, for we have to embody in it proposals for the consolidation of existing achievements.'*
>
> H. Morrison on the nature of the programme to follow *Let Us Face the Future. 1948 Labour Party Conference Report*, p. 122.

Part One: The Background, Campaign and Results

Serious speculation about the date of the next general election began after devaluation in September 1949.[1] The devaluation debates in Parliament were pervaded by an atmosphere of electioneering, particularly from the Conservative side. Although the Cabinet decided on 13 October to announce that there would be no election in 1949, the electioneering atmosphere was maintained in the autumn of 1949 by an extension of the business lobby's anti-nationalisation campaign. Tate and Lyle, the dominant sugar refiner, ran an especially ingenious and vigorous campaign; it also sought to appeal to its workers by offering profit-sharing agreements.[2] Some leading members of the government, notably Morrison, were afflicted by mild hysteria over the campaign,[3] and in October 1949 the NEC asked the Secretary to look into the campaign's effects.

However, this was not a major factor behind Attlee's announcement on 11 January that the country would go to the polls on 23 February. The economy was the most important reason for an early decision. Delay seemed to be having harmful effects on trade, industry and the pound. Cripps also believed that delay might mean pressure for an 'election' budget; this intensely moral man was keen to avoid such pressures. Labour had additionally by late 1949 enacted all the main bills specifically promised in the 1945 manifesto, and the party had agreed on a new programme for a further five-year term of office. Therefore in the month

of the party's fiftieth anniversary, Britain went to the polls to cast judgement on the first Labour majority government.[4]

As early as October 1946 the Research Department had drawn up a
statement for the NEC Policy Sub Committee on the next election. This
foresaw several difficulties in the production of a new programme. *Let Us
Face the Future*, it argued, contained the results of two decades' thinking
when the party was mainly in opposition. Furthermore, it was not clear
what the results of some of Labour's reforms would be. Even so, the
Research Department suggested initiating discussion of key problems,
such as candidates for further nationalisation, the role of incentives in a
full employment economy, the need for change in the machinery of
government, and so on. The Policy Sub Committee agreed to begin this
discussion, and during 1947 several documents were produced and discussed.

Morrison, the Chairman of the Policy and Publicity Sub Committee,
as the Policy Sub Committee became known in 1948, was the dominant
figure behind much of this work, although it would be wrong to ignore the
fact that his views corresponded well with those of many important
individuals and interests in the party. Morrison believed that the 1945
result had confirmed his view that a relatively moderate appeal would
attract the middle class. He therefore sought to commit the party to a
policy which involved consolidation rather than innovation.[5]

Not everyone supported this rejection of a radical line. Bevan and the
left in particular sought more nationalisation on the domestic front. This
was seen as a necessary part of the movement towards the 'Socialist
Commonwealth of Great Britain', promised in *Let Us Face the Future*.
Such policies were not seen as an electoral handicap. Bevan and others
on the left rejected opinion poll evidence which supported the Morrisonian
case. As the *Tribune* noted on 13 January 1950, opinion polls were
mainly 'material for reactionary propaganda' and grossly inaccurate.
Bevan and other members of the left believed in the existence of a radical
working class, or at least a potentially radical electorate.[6]

Supporters of further nationalisation pushed the 'shopping list' approach,
believing that any more general approach would allow Morrison and the
opponents of further nationalisation to escape specific commitments.
The main industries which featured on this list were aircraft, chemicals,
industrial insurance (a form of life insurance), cotton, motors, oil distribution, shipbuilding and water supply. The shopping-list approach
also suited the traditional Labour tendency to advocate such reforms
on essentially pragmatic grounds, especially efficiency. Nevertheless, this

approach made it virtually certain that the more general philosophy of nationalisation would not be examined, and allowed specific objections to emerge for some industries.

During late 1948 a series of policy committees produced a vast amount of material, although quantity rather than quality was the keynote. Consultations took place with the TUC and Cooperative movement. Labour policy was still very much developed with an eye to the unions, as can be seen from the absence of any serious discussion of wages policy. However, whereas the 1945 nationalisation proposals had been evolved in close consultation with the unions, and usually reflected the desire of a specific union to nationalise its 'own' industry, this was not the case in 1948. The support for further nationalisation came more from political quarters, and it was clear that many within the union leadership were not happy about the new proposals. In private industry wages and conditions were improving, while in the nationalised industries there had been far from the salvation expected by some.

In January 1949 the Policy and Publicity Sub Committee approved a general draft statement to be put to the NEC. It decided that the cost of living, food, and homes were the 'three questions of greatest concern in the country', and that they should be the centrepiece of the document. Proposals for the nationalisation of further industries 'should be related to these vital questions', the committee adding that 'We must recognise that the spiritual results of nationalisation are not as good as we hoped'; nationalisation was being pushed even more into an efficiency straightjacket, though a small shopping list remained.

This draft was discussed by the NEC at a joint Cabinet-NEC meeting in February; it was finally approved by the NEC in March. On 23 March a slightly revised version was issued to the party under the title *Labour Believes in Britain*. The most notable features of this statement were proposals to nationalise the cement industry, industrial assurance (the last main element of the Beveridge Report which had not been enacted), meat distribution, sugar refining, and water supply. It also included a promise to examine the chemical industry, and set up a development council for shipping. A continued role for private enterprise was envisaged, but competitive public enterprise was promised to keep the private sector up to maximum efficiency. For the rest, the statement mainly consisted of an exposition of Labour's record.

E. Eldon Barry has argued that the statement contained the 'most rational argument for nationalisation ever put up by the Labour Party', that it challenged 'some of the most powerful capitalist concerns in

Britain'.[7] Certainly the proposals were related to specific arguments; for example, cement was linked to the housing programme and the fact that it was a monopoly; industrial assurance was linked to wasteful competition and the whole insurance system. However, the programme again did not strike at the central financial institutions, or put forward a clear strategy. It remained piecemeal. There was still no serious consideration of the relationship between the public and private sector. Moreover, it is important not to put too much emphasis on the nationalisation proposals in the programme, Consolidation rather than reform was very much the central theme. David Low caught the tone well in a cartoon in the *Evening Chronicle* in April 1949; it depicted Morrison as a shopkeeper selling 'Labour Conservatism'.

Labour Believes in Britain was accepted without serious criticism at the 1949 Labour conference, though it was clear that many on the left opposed its consolidationist approach. Behind the scenes, moderates sought to limit the programme even more. The proposal to nationalise industrial assurance in particular did not please the National Federation of Insurance Workers, and the Cooperative movement, whose Cooperative Insurance Society was a major insurer: it claimed that its insurance was efficient and already socially owned.[8] This combination of moderate, union and Cooperative forces led in November to a major argument in the NEC. A Dalton attempt to drop nationalisation was defeated, but so too was a Bevan motion proposing the retention of nationalisation. Instead, a compromise was reached by which insurance was to be 'mutualised', a conveniently vague term.

The 1950 Labour manifesto was called *Let Us Win Through Together*. It claimed that 'all the main proposals' in *Let Us Face the Future* had been implemented, especially stressing full employment and reforms such as the NHS. These achievements, it was argued, had 'laid the foundations of a future based on free social democracy.' The manifesto promised to maintain these benefits, and seek further progress, particularly in house building. Although it claimed that 'Socialism is not bread alone', efficiency remained the key theme, if not word. The manifesto called for increased production, lower costs, more exports, and so on. Nationalisation, to the extent it figured at all, was mainly presented in these terms. Sugar refining and cement were to be nationalised because they were monopolies; meat distribution and water supply were to become public services. The chemical industry was to be examined; industrial assurance was to be placed under 'mutual' ownership. The manifesto ended with a section on colonial and foreign policy, which promised a vague internationalism and the pursuit of a policy of colonial development.

The Labour campaign reflected the nature of Labour's appeal even more closely than the content of the manifesto. It was an appeal to moderation, to the interests and values of decency and simplicity. It was a campaign in which Attlee made a 1,000-mile speaking tour in his pre-war family saloon, with Mrs Attlee at the wheel. It was a campaign in which the achievement of full employment figured prominently; in which Labour's social reforms were proudly presented. Nationalisation, both past and future, was played down. The old Labour faithful – the iniquities of the inter-war Conservative Party   was played up, and dire warnings were given of the consequences of returning another Conservative government.

The Conservatives sought hard to counter this Labour campaign, and were well prepared to do so. During 1945-1950 the Conservatives undertook a major review of party organisation and policy, with the intention of producing a modern Conservative Party image, which would be largely immune from Labour's mythical atavistic Conservative monster.[9] Lord Woolton, the Chairman of the party, set about an organisational reform, which sought to minimise the role of money in the selection of candidates, make constituency parties more democratic, recruit more qualified agents, and promote party organisation and research in general. He also negotiated the effective integration of the Conservatives and National Liberals. R. A. Butler, who had been the minister responsible for the 1944 Education Act, led a team of mainly younger Conservatives in the production of a new Conservative domestic policy, the best known part of which was the *Industrial Charter*. The details of this programme are not so important as the general desire – namely, to produce an economic policy which rejected *laissez faire* and accepted much of Labour's welfare legislation and interventionism, but at the same time remained committed to an essentially private enterprise economy and to individual freedom.

This new Conservative synthesis, which in many ways harked back to an old Tory paternalism, can be seen clearly in a speech which Churchill, who had played no significant part in this policy reformulation, made in July 1949. The *Manchester Guardian* called the policy 'Tory Socialism'; a reversion to a Disraelian pragmatic-interventionist-reformist Conservatism would be a more accurate, though awkward, epithet.

This policy can be seen even more clearly in the 1950 election manifesto. The manifesto, entitled *This Is the Road*, claimed that Conservative policy was 'to restore to our country her economic independence and to our citizens their full personal freedom and power of initiative'. It claimed that Labour's controls had brought muddle, especially over housing, and contributed to inflation. Full employment, it argued, was a result of Marshall aid, and had nothing to do with specifically Labour policies. The Conservatives could therefore maintain full employment; they would also accept Labour reforms such as the NHS. Road transport and iron and steel, however, would be denationalised. Finally, there was a large degree of agreement over colonial and foreign policy, though Labour was attacked for failing to promote British leadership, particularly in the fields of Commonwealth and European unity.

The Conservative campaign mirrored this manifesto closely. The Conservatives also sought more forcefully to stress their old theme of being the party of all classes and the whole nation; this was often contrasted with alleged 'class war' statements made by Labour leaders, particularly Bevan's 'vermin' speech.

Several smaller parties contested the election, notably the Liberals and communists. The Liberal programme included strong opposition to further nationalisation, though it supported profit sharing and radical measures such as separate parliaments for Scotland and Wales, and equal pay for men and women. The Liberal campaign stressed strongly a Gallup poll which indicated that 38 per cent would vote Liberal if they thought the Liberals had a chance of forming a government — a somewhat double-edged line. The Liberals were desperately short of money, but managed to put up their largest number of candidates since 1929 — 475 (compared to the Conservatives' 619 and Labour's 617). The communists made a much more strenuous effort to win widespread support than in 1945, strongly challenging Labour's record and putting up 100 candidates.

The result of the election was a narrow Labour victory. Labour won 315 seats and 46.1 per cent of the poll, compared to 393 seats and 48.0 per cent in 1945. The Conservatives won 298 seats and 43.5 per cent of the poll, against 210 seats and 39.6 per cent for the National coalition in 1945. The minor parties again fared badly. The Liberals' representation dropped from 12 seats and 9.0 per cent of the vote, to 9 seats and 9.1 per cent (the latter figure representing fewer votes per seat contested); communist representation fell from 2 to 0, and support from 0.4 to 0.3 per cent. The turnout was a massive 83.9 per cent, compared to 72.7 per cent in 1945. The swing to the Conservatives was 2.9 per cent, and Labour was left with a majority of 6.[10]

Part Two: Analysis of the Results

The swing at 2.9 per cent was relatively low, but the evidence is that behind this figure lay a slightly larger movement among former voters; Mass Observation estimated that one in ten Labour voters of 1945 had switched their allegiance. Why did the pendulum swing back against Labour? Several reasons seem important.

In some ways the election must be viewed against the whole background of 1945-1950, and even beyond. Voters' attitudes are usually formed over a long period.

The 1945 defeat had been a shocking one for the Conservatives, but in many ways the party's position remained strong. In terms of the popular vote, the Conservatives remained an important force. They had a leader who was a world figure and greatly respected by large sections of the British people, even if his support was not as great as some assumed. For all the ideological differences in the party, there was no great issue of divide — as tariffs had been after the last great Conservative defeat in 1906. The Conservatives retained the financial support of big business, a support if anything strengthened by Labour's nationalisation programme.

Intellectually, the climate was also far from totally in Labour's favour. Increasing evidence of the horrors of Soviet communism were beginning to have their effects even among those sympathetic to socialism; George Orwell was to testify to this in his novel *1984*, published in 1949. The pre-war support which had existed for *étatisme* and planning, even in quite moderate circles, also began to be challenged. The growth of the role of the state during and after the second world war was used by some to show that socialism was no pipe dream, but for others it marked, to use the title of Professor F.A. Hayek's seminal 1944 tract, *The Road to Serfdom*. Increasingly individual freedom from restraint was being eroded in favour of state power. And this in a western world, unlike in the 1930s, characterised by growing prosperity and economic optimism; indeed, it was all too easy after 1945 to contrast capitalist America and its riches with socialist Britain and its rationing, its shortages.

During 1945-1950 the Conservatives also made great efforts to improve their organisation, choose 'target' constituencies, and so on. Although it is doubtful whether organisation was a major factor, it almost certainly helped the Conservatives gain a few extra seats, especially as a result of the introduction of postal voting.

During 1945-1950 Conservative confidence and unity were also helped by the problems which afflicted Labour, particularly during and after

1947. It was certainly during 1947 that the Conservatives' performance in by-elections began to pick up, and they overtook Labour in opinion polls — though they never won a Parliamentary seat from Labour in any by-election during the whole period. By late 1949 the Conservatives had a massive lead in the opinion polls. In November Gallup gave the Conservatives a 48 per cent rating to Labour's 38 per cent. Another poll in January 1950 showed that Labour had retained only 75 per cent of its 1945 supporters, 10 per cent having deserted to the Conservatives.

What specifically during these years lost Labour votes? Mass Observation found that many of Labour's deserters felt some form of grievance over unsatisfied material expectations. Certainly Labour's losses in 1950 were to be heavy in middle-class dormitory areas, and Mass Observation found during the late 1940s that large numbers of middle-class people felt that they were badly off, a feeling that had some justification as sections of the middle class were increasingly being hit by higher taxes (an average of 34 per cent of personal income was taken by taxes in 1950, compared to 20 per cent in 1938). Comparative class living standards pose tricky problems, but one study in 1948 estimated that the real standard of living of parts of the middle class may even have fallen during the previous ten years, whereas the urban workers' living standards rose by approximately 20 per cent.[11]

These, and other, problems were made worse by bad government public relations. Many have claimed that the public at this time took a great deal of interest in politics; Dalton was later to write that Parliament 'was a living and dramatic spectacle, successfully challenging competition with other forms of entertainment'.[12] The truth is somewhat different. Interest was undoubtedly relatively high, though Parliament, or politics in general, was hardly entertainment, unless providing jokes for comedians is counted. Moreover, there is widespread evidence that people felt uninformed about government plans. As early as October 1945 Gallup found that 50 per cent thought that the government was not telling the people enough about its policies, and only 29 per cent that it was.

While the peacetime role of the government increased rapidly, Labour allowed government information services to decline in size and importance. On 6 December 1945 the Cabinet discussed the Ministry of Information, the wartime propaganda organisation; Attlee argued that it was 'politically dangerous that there should be a Minister with no other responsibility but the conduct of publicity'. After discussion, the Ministry of Information was wound up, and a Central Office of Information set up, with a more restricted budget and mandate. Subsequently, economic crises and

Conservative criticism led to further cuts in the budget — and this at a time of growing business expenditure on propaganda!

In the 1947 Economic Survey it was stated that the government was going to take the people into its confidence, no matter how 'difficult the situation may be'. However, the main medium was the printed word rather than the new media of film and radio, though the government made quite extensive use of ministerial statements in newsreels (which at the time had a weekly audience of over 20 million). There were good reasons for this, such as the statutory impartiality of the BBC, but this concentration on the written word, and pedestrian newsreel presentations, limited the publicity's effects. Mass Observation found that these campaigns had little impact in any widespread sense; it argued that the language and presentation were wrong, that ordinary people did not understand, even if they read the material   a conclusion borne out by the government's own Social Survey. Labour made some efforts to use ordinary language; for example, a civil servant in 1948 advised Cripps to speak of a 'Household Budget' in his radio broadcast on the Economic Survey. But this preference for Anglo-Saxon over Latin was rare among the Oxbridge classics-dominated higher civil service, and in government publicity in general.

The Labour Party, like the government, also never paid careful enough attention to the media and the message during 1945-1950. Its propaganda media were traditional: the meeting, the pamphlet — media which reached only a limited audience. At the same time, the Conservatives and pressure groups were experimenting with more varied media, and using polling organisations to advise them on the content of their message and its effectiveness.

The government's and Labour's message also failed to differentiate Labour policy from existing values. The appeal for the 'Dunkirk spirit' was common; George Isaacs, the Minister of Labour, claimed in a Movietone newsreel in 1946 that he was loath to invoke the Dunkirk spirit, but went on to do so! Other ministers found it equally easy to lapse into such language. The popular version of the 1947 Economic Survey was called 'The Battle for Output', and this emphasis on production, or more generally harder work and efficiency, pervaded much government and Labour Party publicity. Production and other economic goals were clearly important, but Labour failed to relate its economic aims to more general socialist aims. Indeed, often its publicity seemed to be implying that it was simply seeking a more efficient form of capitalism. The myths, the rhetoric, the crusading zeal of the party's early days, and even as late as the war years, were largely gone by 1950.

The election campaign itself in 1950 saw Labour alter a Conservative lead of 6 per cent in opinion polls to a Labour lead of 1.5 per cent. As in 1945, the most common arguments relating to the campaign indicated a swing in the opposite direction, again emphasising that the major factors behind the result were medium and long-term ones.

Many commentators have claimed that Labour's campaign harped on issues which no longer concerned the electorate, or on issues which, in David Howell's words, formed part of 'the emerging consensus on economic and social policy'.[13] Certainly the fear of unemployment and memories of mass unemployment in the inter-war years were not the potent forces they had been in 1945, except perhaps in some areas of former high unemployment. Labour's social reforms had been popular, but they were not seen by many as a significant issue in the election; again memories and myths of an antediluvian Conservative Party were losing their force. Housing remained the most important issue for electors, though the number mentioning it as the most important issue had fallen from 41 per cent in 1945 to 27 per cent; Labour now found itself in the position of having to defend its record on this problematic issue. Labour also found itself in trouble over nationalisation. Although Labour played down the issue, the Conservatives, and previously pressure groups, played it up. In 1950 22 per cent considered nationalisation the most important issue in the election, second only to housing, and a vast increase over nationalisation's 6 per cent rating in 1945. Also, a considerable number rating nationalisation most important in 1950 were hostile to further nationalisation, whereas in 1945 there had been general support. The Conservatives were on firm ground too in concentrating on the cost of living, rising taxation, and government expenditure, which was 37 per cent of gross national product in 1950, compared to 26 per cent in 1938.

The mass media if anything offered Labour fewer advantages than in 1945. There was a strong belief in the Labour Party that the press was biased against it, and this helped lead in 1947 to the appointment of a Royal Commission on the press. The Commission reported in 1949 that there was nowhere near a monopoly of ownership or opinion, and that the low standards of many papers were mainly a reflection of public taste. Radical changes, such as state finance, were rejected. However, Labour's main support came from the *Daily Herald* and *Daily Mirror*, whereas the Tories could marshall a vast array of papers. By 1950 the BBC was also under attack from Labour for alleged Conservative bias, a more accurate claim than the Conservatives' charges of Labour bias in 1945,[14] though the Beveridge Committee on broadcasting, appointed in 1949, basically defended the position of the BBC, ignoring the lack of access of dissenting groups to this source of conservative social influence. During the 1950 campaign the BBC again carried party political broadcasts, although fewer than in 1945, and they were listened to by fewer people. The Conservatives, who generally accepted that Labour's broadcasts in 1945 had been better, paid particular attention to their presentation in 1950, producing a more polished set of broadcasts. However, again there is not much evidence that the media were a major factor, at least in the short run.

A last point concerns the electoral system. Overall, Labour received 50.4 per cent of the seats for 46.1 per cent of the vote, a much more proportional result than in 1945. More specifically, certain aspects of the system gave a considerable advantage to the Conservatives, whereas in 1945 the tendency had been the other way. The Representation of the People Acts of 1948 and 1949 introduced several important changes.[15] First was postal voting, estimated to have added 1-2 per cent to the poll: Morrison claimed that this vote was cast 10-1 against Labour, and others have argued that it was worth ten seats plus to the Conservatives. There was also a major redistribution of seats, leaving Labour with 50 of the 60 largest majorities; Labour's Secretary estimated that this was worth 30 seats to the Conservatives, again a figure confirmed by other sources.[16] These changes more than made up for Conservative losses resulting from the end of plural voting. But then the high poll, on a new register, must have helped Labour, as opinion polls showed that Labour continued to have an advantage among 'don't knows' and probable non-voters. Liberal candidatures also again had their effects. Polls showed that Liberals continued to prefer the Conservatives to Labour, so the fact that the Liberals did not contest all seats helped the Conservatives more than Labour. However, the Liberals contested more seats than in 1945; their increased vote may therefore have come more from the Conservatives than Labour, although the increase in the poll could account for it.

So how can the 1950 general election be summed up? What was the social composition of the vote, and what were the views of the electorate compared to 1945?

Socially, Labour retained strong support among young voters, and among men, especially trade unionists, though women were showing an increasing tendency to vote Labour. Labour undoubtedly suffered losses among the middle class; in 1945 Gallup found that 21 per cent of the middle class claimed to be Labour, and 54 per cent Conservative; by 1950 these figures had become 16 and 63 per cent. However, Labour retained its working-class vote; Gallup found that the same proportion of the working class was voting Conservative as in 1945 — approximately 30 per cent. Many have argued that the middle class was alienated by Bevan's 'vermin' speech, and other Labour 'class' statements.[17] Almost certainly more important was the fact that the middle class had gained little benefit from full employment, but had felt harmed by high taxes and rising prices. Mass Observation's work certainly confirmed this. (It also discovered growing hostility to the unions, although the unions were not always equated with the Labour Party.) On the other hand, many working-class people had done well out of the Labour government; class consciousness remained strong, and the identification with Labour stronger than ever. Mass Observation found that 47 per cent of Labour voters gave class reasons for their preference, compared to 43 per cent in 1945; no other specific factor was mentioned to any significant extent.

In terms of the views of the electorate, there can be little doubt that it was essentially conservative. In 1950 most people wanted to conserve what had been achieved during 1945-1950. The main arguments and problems concerned which party was most likely to conserve the benefits, and provide new ones. The Labour Secretary in his report on the election to the NEC in March 1950 noted that industrial workers had voted Labour more strongly than ever before because Labour had delivered full employment, more equality, social services, and so on. He claimed that the middle class had been lost because of a fear that it was relatively declining in material terms, and frustration among potential owner-occupiers. A further interesting comment on the views of the electorate is to be found in a Policy and Publicity Sub Committee memorandum of May 1950. This also noted that Labour more than ever was attracting a mass working-class vote, but accepted that this was not a socialist electorate, that 'We have a big task ahead in converting the workers'.

Beer has argued that there was a weakening 'of Socialist commitment' during this period, and that this was caused by growing affluence.[18] However, this is in part a misreading of the mood of 1945, and subsequent events. In 1945 there had been a widespread desire for change, but this desire was often vague and not necessarily socialist. During 1945-1950 opinion polls showed an increasing number thinking the government 'Too Socialist', and by 1950 few sought radical change (figures for the last questionnaire, in November 1949, showed that 48 per cent thought the government too socialist, 27 per cent about right, and 12 per cent not socialist enough). Nevertheless, to attribute this simply to growing affluence seems unwarranted; undoubtedly more complex factors were at work. One of these was the nature of Labour's presentation of socialism and its policies, in particular its increasing tendency to play down the ethical side of socialism.

In 1945 the result had lent itself to a variety of interpretations, but in the euphoria of victory it was to be some time before this debate gathered momentum in the party. The 1950 result was also to lend itself to varying analyses, but with another election clearly imminent, the debate on future electoral strategy was to begin almost as soon as the votes were counted.

Chapter Eight

GOVERNING THE 'NEW' BRITAIN (AGAIN)

'CRA says we should carry on, since we have a majority, even though a bare half dozen . . . Most think — and I most emphatically — that this Parliament can't last more than a few months.'

Dalton Diaries, 25 February 1950.

Part One: Cabinet Making and Government

Late on the Friday evening after the 1950 general election, when it had become clear that Labour had been returned with a bare majority, the Cabinet met to consider the situation. The decision was to carry on in government. A few minor changes were made, but basically the same team continued to govern the 'new' Britain.

The Cabinet contained eighteen members, two fewer than in 1945. Again it included representatives of the various ideologies and interests in the party. The left remained under-represented, and, unlike in 1945, the unions were also under-represented. In 1945 there had been six trade unionists in the Cabinet, while in 1950 there were only four; at the same time, the proportion of union-sponsored members of the PLP had risen.[1] This decline was a cause of concern for Attlee and many leading unionists, but several trade unionist ministers during 1945-1950 had proved less than competent: for example, Isaacs at the Ministry of Labour needed briefing down to the last comma. Some trade unionists proved good ministers, and there were non-unionists who proved poor ministers, but the unions' tendency not to sponsor their best men for Parliament meant that there was a shortage of ministerial talent among this group.

The structure of government remained essentially unchanged. Cabinet committees continued on a large scale, though there had been some criticism from ministers during 1945-1950 on account of these committees taking up too much time, and more personally, that Morrison tended to interfere too often. Attlee continued to make use of what amounted to an inner Cabinet, including especially Bevin and Cripps, though after their resignations in 1950 and 1951 through ill health Attlee became more aloof.

Attlee considered making some departmental changes, in particular separating the Ministry of Health from local government and housing, adding these to Town and Country Planning. It is not clear why Attlee did not follow these lines, though he did in 1951 separate health from local government and housing. Probably the main reason was Bevan, who was losing interest in his ministry, but who could not be fitted in elsewhere with a ministry of sufficient standing to suit his taste. There was also little need for such mergers on policy grounds, as Labour was not planning any major new legislation, though mergers would have offered administrative advantages.

Part Two: Parliament and Party

The absence of any new major reform proposals in part reflected a widespread belief in the government that Labour's Parliamentary majority was unsure. The probability of another election in the near future meant that the Lords was likely to veto any radical legislation, and even the new Parliament Act meant that such a veto would impose at least a year's delay — until probably after the next election. Labour's majority of six entitled it to only a fraction of one majority on standing committees. Initially, committees were staffed by an equal number of Labour and opposition members, though Labour was later given a majority of one. It quickly became evident that it was possible to govern with a small majority, though the strain on MPs was considerable. Nevertheless, Labour made no effort to introduce radical new legislation; party divisions and the prospect of a Lords veto made such action difficult, even pointless.

The Conservatives continually harried the government. The main issue of domestic contention was the government's insistence on proceeding with iron and steel nationalisation. On three occasions the opposition introduced what amounted to motions of censure, but the government wheeled out its palsied and lame, and scraped through.

Labour's Parliamentary party organisation remained basically the same as it was during 1945-1950. The small majority had one advantage for Labour in that it helped maintain discipline, in spite of serious differences of opinion within the party over foreign, defence, and future domestic policy. Even after Bevan's resignation over the budget in 1951, and with growing troubles over foreign policy, dissent in Parliament remained muted, though there was some discontent in the party outside Parliament as Labour groped for a new *raison d'être*.

Relations with the party outside Parliament had not been entirely peaceful even during 1945-1950. Conference on the whole was quiescent as Labour enacted its programme. Nevertheless, there were some notable attacks on government policy, especially from the unions, though there was no united block vote, or union-constituency split. It has often been claimed that Bevin could always rely on the unswerving support of the union block votes,[2] but there was considerable criticism of foreign policy from this quarter on occasions. Conference also saw mounting attacks on nationalisation, particularly over the public corporation format. However, these criticisms achieved little. Indeed, a classic example of the leadership ignoring conference decisions comes from this time. In 1947 conference voted by 1,558,000 to 1,550,000 to end the practice of the tied cottage. Bevan, the minister responsible, and the government did nothing.

Miliband has argued that the key to the government-rank and file relations at this time lies not in constitutional niceties, but in the radical desires of the rank and file, and moderation of the Labour leadership.[3] Certainly the left was better represented among the rank and file than in the government, though it is wrong to think that all, or even a significant number of the rank and file was left-wing. Moreover, it is important to realise that the leadership was moved not only by a view of constitutional proprieties, but also by a belief that conference was in many ways neither democratic nor representative. Increasing infiltration of constituency parties by communists and others on the left, together with growing communist activities in the unions,[4] added to fears about conference (and provided the leadership with a more credible communist bogy to damn policies it did not like, for example opposition to wages policy).

During 1945-1950 there were some criticisms of this subordination of the non-Parliamentary party. Laski frequently criticised the regulation of the NEC from the leading role which he had hoped it would play in 1945; the NEC itself in February 1948 considered a memorandum attacking the subjugation of conference. However, these general attacks were no more successful than the specific ones at conference.

Nevertheless, the government during 1945-1950 was not completely immune from party pressure, especially from the unions. The unions remained the main financial support for the party. In 1945 they contributed £111,154 to the election fund, while other sources could muster only £14,284; in 1950 the figures were £156,178 and £15,603 respectively.[5] The reintroduction of contracting out of the political levy, and growing membership, led to a vast increase in affiliated membership, from 2,510,000 in 1945 to 4,972,000 in 1950. Individual membership also rose dramatically, from 487,047 in 1945 to an apogee of 908,161 in 1950, but proportionately the union strength at conference was increased. Naturally, this meant that the unions remained a major influence within the party.

During 1945-1950 union leaders worked behind the scenes against certain Labour policies they did not like, and in an attempt to ensure greater cooperation by the government. However, relations remained essentially good. There was a strong sense of loyalty to the government, which was implementing many policies the unions had supported for many years. Moreover, the new union leadership which emerged after 1945 remained moderate. Certainly Victor Tewson, who succeeded Citrine as General Secretary of the TUC, and Arthur Deakin, Bevin's successor at the TGWU, were restrained in their dealing with the government in general. For example, in Cabinet on 17 July 1947 Morrison reported that over wages policy the union leaders had 'shown a considerable sense of responsibility', though adding that 'a great deal remains to be done in educating the rank and file'. At the same time, Bevin continued to take an interest in union affairs, thus easing government-union relations over issues such as using troops in strikes.[6]

In his cartoons, Low portrayed the TUC as an old carthourse, somewhat behind the times, slow, but basically reliable. It is a picture which encapsulates the union-government relationship during this period, though the unions became more assertive after 1950, especially over opposition to further nationalisation and wages policy — a development which heralded a renewal of tension between the industrial and political wings of the party.

Chapter Nine

THE 1950-1951 GOVERNMENT

*'I feel bound to tell you that for my part I think
the appointment of Gaitskell to be a great mistake.
I should have thought myself that it was essential
to find out whether the holder of this great office
would commend himself to the main elements
and currents of opinion in the Party. After all,
the policies which he will have to propound and
carry out are bound to have the most profound
and important repercussions throughout the
movement.'*

A. Bevan to C.R. Attlee on the appointment of
H. Gaitskell as Chancellor of the Exchequer,
October 1950. Bevan Papers.

Part One: Foreign, Defence and Colonial Policy

During 1950-1951 external affairs, especially the Korean war and its
implications, increasingly came to dominate the thinking of the government, and to a lesser extent the electorate. At the same time, these
developments further divided the Labour Party.

In June 1950 the government of South Korea claimed that the country
had been invaded by troops from communist North Korea. The Americans
agreed to send help, calling on their allies for support. The British government had no hesitation in complying; there were strong fears that the
Soviet Union was preparing aggression elsewhere, that America's commitment to the defence of Europe might be in doubt if support was less
than wholehearted. The war rapidly escalated, and troops from the new
Chinese communist state became involved. Many have claimed that the
British exercised an important restraining influence on America, and that
in particular a trip made by Attlee to America in December 1950 helped
persuade Truman not to use atomic weapons.[1] Certainly the British view
of south east Asia was different to the American one; Bevin showed in
a Cabinet paper as early as 1948 that he did not accept the American

line that communist China was a Russian pawn, and Britain recognised red China before the Korean war began — although this in part reflected a desire to safeguard British economic interests, and to keep in step with Asian members of the Commonwealth. There is no doubt that the British government advised caution. Nevertheless, there is little evidence that British attitudes had an important effect on American policy.

During the Korean crisis Morrison came to take a growing interest in foreign affairs. As the UN commander, General MacArthur, pushed on towards China in late 1950 Morrison urged peace initiatives. Morrison previously had not been greatly interested in foreign affairs, though there is evidence that he hoped to be Foreign Secretary in 1945. In March 1951 Bevin's continuing illness led Attlee, who had frequently been forced to double as Foreign Secretary, to ask Bevin to resign. He was replaced by Morrison — much to Bevin's disgust (Bevin died a month later).

Although many welcomed the appointment at the time, subsequently the choice of a man who could reportedly say that 'foreign policy would be OK except for bloody foreigners' was to be strongly criticised. Attlee has described it as the worst decision which he made: 'I didn't know he knew so little.'[2] But Attlee had little choice. Dalton made it clear that he was not a candidate; his reasons for this are not entirely clear, but almost certainly he knew enough about foreign affairs not to seek the job at so troubled a time. He recommended James Griffiths, who had been appointed Colonial Secretary in 1950; he was a trade unionist, and Attlee was keen to see unionists in major posts to maintain a balance of interests in the government. Nevertheless, Griffiths was not thought to be suitably qualified, or of sufficient stature. The same was true of Bevan.[3] Morrison was pressing his own case strongly; he still aspired to lead the Labour Party, and experience in another field of government would be useful.

During his period as Foreign Secretary Morrison faced serious problems; to some extent he was a victim of bad luck; and ultimately only Morrison's reputation suffered. For a time Attlee was ill; Morrison had to double as Prime Minister when his party was showing growing divisive tendencies; furthermore his wife was dying. Morrison had the misfortune to follow Bevin, who had generally been considered a success, and who got on well with his advisers. Morrison did not get on with most of his Foreign Office staff. Their innate sense of superiority brought out his feeling of inferiority; he disliked their formality. They disliked his concern with domestic policy, his love of Parliament, his hectoring, and refusal to treat the Foreign Office as something special. Morrison tended to ignore Foreign Office briefs, and to some extent his officials snidely smeared him in return.[4] True, he was a less than impressive Foreign Secretary. Even so, it is difficult to argue that his tenure of office significantly altered the course of British policy, or harmed the fortunes of the Labour Party.

Morrison's first mission was to Paris for a meeting of the Committee of Ministers of the Council of Europe.[5] The main item on the agenda was whether the Council should be authorised to discuss defence. The British position was hostile; Britain had an Atlantic conception of defence; any serious form of European organisation was further seen as a threat to Parliamentary sovereignty. Morrison, a great Parliamentarian and believer in Empire, had little time for 'Europe'. Although he had led the Labour delegation to the Council of Europe in 1949, in Cabinet in January 1951 he advocated British withdrawal. This had run into strong opposition even from other anti-Europeans. In particular, Bevin had stressed the need not to create tensions before Germany was rearmed and admitted to NATO.[6]

German rearmament had become a serious issue since the outset of the Korean war. There was growing pressure from America to admit West Germany into the western defence orbit; acceptance of this was made a condition for sending reinforcements. M.R. Gordon has argued that Labour accepted German rearmament without the 'slightest trace' of 'socialist hostility to militarism'.[7] However, Bevin agreed in principle only reluctantly, and major divisions remained in the Cabinet and in the party at large. There were also divisions over a plan put forward by the French in 1950 for a European Defence Community. Bevin rejected this plan outright, and Morrison was initially opposed, though by the time of the 1951 general election he was becoming more sympathetic.

Britian also remained opposed to any major form of European economic cooperation. Bevin had worked hard to promote unity in continental Europe, especially Franco-German *rapprochement*, but he had never assumed that Britain would be part of that unity. In April 1950 he had circulated a document, written by Ernest Davies, on what were called 'regional organisations'. The document was hostile, arguing that cooperation should only be given if all governments had socialist economies. Otherwise, it was claimed, there would be a threat to socialism and the planned economy in Britain. Dalton and others strongly supported this line.

These attitudes very much conditioned Britain's response to a French proposal in May 1950 for a European Coal and Steel Community, out of which was later to emerge the Common Market. Bevin felt that Britain had been kept in the dark, and that the plan was designed to exclude Britain anyway.[8] The coal and steel industries had been nationalised by Labour, so the government was loath to hand them over to a supranational authority. The miners were strongly opposed, and in June 1950 the NEC published a pamphlet entitled *European Unity*, which opposed British participation. Britain therefore declined to join the new organisation. This policy was strongly supported by Morrison, though towards the end of the government he became more sympathetic to Europe, and increasingly aware of Britain's reliance on the United States.

By this time Morrison had become preoccupied with the crisis which developed in 1951 over the Anglo-Iranian Oil Company. £350 million of British capital was invested in the company; over a quarter of Britain's crude oil supplies in 1950 came from the company. These were the sort of interests which had troubled Labour in earlier dealings with the Arabs, and heightened fears of Soviet expansionism. In April 1951 the fervent nationalist Dr Mossadeq became Iranian Prime Minister. Shortly afterwards the Anglo-Iranian Oil Company was nationalised, and anti-British rioting broke out. At the same time, the situation in Egypt was deteriorating over Britain's continued military presence there.

Morrison gave the impression initially that he was not fully dealing with the problem, that he was more concerned with launching the Festival of Britain and other affairs. Britain simply protested, and submitted her case to the International Court of Justice at the Hague. From the end of May the Cabinet was willing to concede the principle of nationalisation, provided there was a negotiated settlement, and a guarantee of the flow of oil. But Britain also strengthened her forces in the eastern Mediterranean and threatened to withdraw all personnel from the Abadan refinery, a policy which involved an element of bluff as Britain needed the oil.

Morrison was quite hawkish and jingoist, though the general Foreign Office line was conciliatory, but in late June in a Commons debate he inflamed party tensions by accusing the Conservatives of imperialism, of seeking military intervention. He further did nothing to inspire confidence in his handling of the affair by his inability to pronounce names like Euphrates, which Morrison said as two syllables. Bevin too had trouble pronouncing foreign words, but as one wit noted at the time, at least he knew where the places were. Morrison's handling of the crisis was increasingly making him a target of ridicule and attack.

An emergency mission was sent to Iran under Richard Stokes, the Lord Privy Seal, but on 31 July the Abadan refinery ceased working and Stokes was recalled. In September the Cabinet considered military action.

Morrison supported this; Attlee, who had been conducting foreign policy while Morrison was in America, was cautious. Attlee preferred to work through the UN, pointing out that Truman had not promised American aid. Morrison had little time for the UN, considering it an impractical talking shop. Nevertheless, Attlee carried the day. During October, which also saw Egyptian unilateral abrogation of the 1936 treaty with Britain, British personnel were withdrawn from Abadan. They returned blaming Morrison and the British government for weakness and vacillation.

Morrison had not handled the situation well, but it is doubtful if the British government could have pursued any other constructive course. The affair provided the Conservatives with ammunition to attack Morrison and the government. On the other hand, it allowed Morrison and others to develop the warmonger theme against the Conservatives. Morrison unquestionably suffered from the affair personally, but the guilty party was more the Anglo-Iranian Oil Company, for not coming to a fairer deal with the Iranians before, and therefore helping to fuel nationalist sentiment.

During the discussions over military action it had become clear that in spite of the massive rearmament programme begun in 1950 as a result of the Korean war, it was far from clear that Britain could undertake such an expedition, and that much depended on the Americans' attitude. On 12 September 1950 Attlee had announced a defence programme of £3,600,000 for 1951-1954, a target raised in January 1951 to £4,700,000. Labour had already been spending a high percentage of gross national product on defence, in spite of cutbacks since 1945; indeed, its per capita estimates for 1950-1951 were higher than those of America! The American government and British Chiefs of Staff had pressed for an expenditure of £6,000 million, or 14 per cent of gross national product, so the January 1951 programme represented a considerable cut in these demands. Nevertheless, the rearmament programme was strongly opposed in the Labour Party, especially by Bevan and the left, and played a part in Bevan's resignation over the 1951 budget.[9] It was unquestionably doubtful whether the programme was well advised, particularly in view of its domestic economic effects. Labour's main defence is that there were considerable fears that a major war was imminent. There were further criticisms over the passage in September 1950 of a National Service Bill, extending conscription to two years.

Against a background of these important developments, colonial affairs naturally took something of a back seat. The new Colonial Secretary, James Griffiths, the former Minister of National Insurance, was a

man with no detailed knowledge of colonial affairs. Dalton, a more suitable choice in terms of knowledge, declined the office, confiding to his
diary that likely troubles from 'nigger communities' and reactionary
whites did not appeal to him. He wrote to Attlee stating that Bevan
wanted the job, but Griffiths was preferred. He had been a sound minister,
and was considered a safer choice than the erratic Bevan, who Attlee saw
as colour-prejudiced — 'pro-black, and anti-white'. The main policy developments were the Colombo Plan, signed in November 1950, and the
establishment of a Central African Federation, both of which had implications much wider than colonial policy, and the former owed much to
Bevin.[10]

In the 1951 *Tribune* pamphlet *One Way Only*, the needs of development aid were pushed over those of British defence and rearmament. It
argued 'We have made a start in applying the principles of fair shares in
these islands, although there is still a long way to go before we can claim
to have established a Socialist society. Our next task is to extend the same
principles of fair shares *between* nations and the tens of millions for whom
poverty is still the greatest enemy.' At the 1951 Labour conference Bevan
claimed that a 'World Plan' to aid poor countries was the 'central issue' of
the election, which Attlee had called for later the same month. Nevertheless, few outside the Labour left echoed this call. Colonial policy, and
the poor nations in general, remained the concern of the few in the Labour
Party, and of hardly anyone among an electorate more interested in
immediate economic conditions.

Part Two: Economic Policy

During 1950 the British economy was beginning to show strong signs of
recovery. Britain was in as healthy a balance of payments position as she
had been since 1945, with a surplus of £307 million, compared to a
deficit of £1 million in 1949, and £230 million deficit in 1946. By
December gold and dollar reserves had improved so much that it was
possible to suspend Marshall aid payments, which from 1948 to 1950
had contributed £2,400 million to Britain. Industrial production continued to improve, standing at 195 in 1950, compared to 183 in 1949,
and 149 in 1946. Wages and prices were fairly stable, prices standing
at 114 in 1950, compared to 111 in 1949; wages stood at 111, compared
to 109 in 1949.

However, during late 1950 and especially 1951 things took a turn for
the worse. The rearmament boom led to stockpiling, especially in the

USA, adding to demand from rapidly growing world industrial production.[11] The terms of trade moved against Britain, import prices rising at over double the rate of export prices, though this in part reflected an inflexible attitude by British manufacturers in responding to changed conditions.[12] This helped produce renewed speculation against the pound, and a balance of payments deficit of £369 million in 1951. Inflation, already fuelled by devaluation, worsened, the price level in 1951 rising to 125. Partly because of this, wages rose sharply too, wage rates standing at 120 in 1951. Continuing full employment also probably contributed slightly to this; unemployment, which had stood at 1.5 per cent in 1950, dropped to 1.2 per cent in 1951, the lowest of any of the peacetime years.

Against this background the government reintroduced some controls. During 1948-1950 Wilson had announced the end of a large number of controls, including in May 1950 the abolition of the points system of allocating inessential goods. An agreement with other OEEC countries in 1949 involved a further liberalisation of trade, and the end of most licensing relating to these countries. This was accompanied by the establishment in July 1950 of a European Payments Union, under which trade deficits between OEEC countries were settled in part through gold payments. British purchases from the OEEC countries as a result rose dramatically, from £575 million to £932 million during 1950-1951, adding to the balance of payments troubles. Further difficulties produced by the Korean war boom led to the reimposition of some controls, and the introduction of new ones. In July 1951 the government announced a limitation on dividends. From 1947-1950, under government exhortation, companies had restricted dividends, but in 1950-1951 dividends increased more rapidly than wages.[13] This new limitation was highly unpopular among businessmen and the Conservatives, though a bill implementing it had not been passed by the time of the 1951 general election. The government additionally made it illegal for companies to transfer overseas if this meant the avoidance of tax liability, though by this time many companies had already left. Nevertheless, the return of certain controls during 1950-1951 showed that the government to some extent realised that exhortation and budgetary policy alone could not run the economy.

The Economic Survey also continued to be published. Indeed, the 1951 Survey was in many ways the most sophisticated produced in terms of technique, a testimony to the growing competence of the planners. However, it discontinued a number of forecasts, and stressed that 'many of the quantitative' statistics were 'tentative and conditional'. It was clear that by this time macro-economic planning was not accorded a major role in government policy.

Budgetary policy remained at the heart of Labour's economic management. The 1950 budget introduced few changes. The 1951 budget sought to impose further austerity measures to help pay for the rearmament programme, and damp demand. Purchase tax was raised, and income tax returned to 9 shillings and sixpence in the pound. To keep the cost of the NHS down, charges were imposed on false teeth and spectacles. To limit dividends, the tax on distributed profits was raised from 30 per cent to 50 per cent. It was also announced that the government was to consider monetary policy more carefully. There had been increasing friction between the banks and government over credit restriction; in his budget speech the Chancellor welcomed some rise in long-term interest rates as a check on investment. Monetary policy was thus being accorded some role, although a subsidiary one to budgetary policy and direct controls.

The 1951 budget was to provoke a major clash between Bevan and Gaitskell, who had been appointed Chancellor of the Exchequer in late 1950. In July 1950 Cripps had again fallen ill, and in October he resigned. Attlee sent for Shinwell to advise him; he recommended Morrison. Attlee disliked this suggestion, thinking Morrison knew nothing about finance; Morrison, remembering how his fingers had been burned while attempting to coordinate economic planning during 1945-1947, did not want the job. Dalton supported Gaitskell, a former economics lecturer and Minister of Economic Affairs since February 1950. More important, Cripps gave the same advice. This accorded with Attlee's thinking, and Gaitskell was appointed the new Chancellor of the Exchequer.[14]

Bevan, who had been close to Cripps, was staggered by the news, a reaction which reflected a mixture of feelings. He felt that leaders of the party should represent something, or somebody; to Bevan, Gaitskell was just a middle-class civil servant, terms of abuse from this Welsh self-styled Marxist member of the proletariat. He felt, to some extent rightly, that Gaitskell would not appeal to the more working-class sections of the party's electorate, and to the more fervently socialist members.[15] However, there is no doubt that Bevan at this time was unsettled at the Ministry of Health. Whilst not seeking to be Chancellor of the Exchequer, for which he had few qualifications, he was unhappy to see Gaitskell promoted before him. These factors helped condition Bevan's relations with Gaitskell in the crisis that was brewing over NHS expenditure.

During 1949 and 1950 there was mounting friction in the government over the rising costs of the NHS; in 1948-1949 there had to be supplementary estimates of £58 million, and in 1949-1950 the figure was £99 million. At first Bevan, who identified strongly with the service, tried to claim that this simply reflected pent up demand resulting from the absence of such free services before 1948, that demand would soon decrease. But a general impression grew up among many ministers that health service expenditure was slipping out of control, and that muddle and extravagance were creeping in,[16] feelings increased by the belief that Bevan was a difficult colleague, irresponsible, and a spendthrift. Therefore in 1950 a Cabinet committee was appointed to review NHS expenditure (expenditure in 1950 was £477 million, 4.4 per cent of national income).

In January 1951 Bevan moved from the Ministry of Health to the Ministry of Labour, but the accusations against the NHS continued, and Bevan's desire to defend it remained just as strong, especially when the attack came from Gaitskell. The pressure for a cut in NHS expenditure was increased by Britain's rearmament drive. Gaitskell, who had even earlier supported cuts, decided to impose a charge on false teeth and spectacles in his 1951 budget. Bevan in 1949 had introduced a Health Service Amendment Act, empowering the levying of a 1 shilling charge for prescriptions. This had never been implemented, but Bevan had not resigned, so he was clearly not opposed to charges in principle. Nevertheless, Gaitskell's decision led to Bevan's departure from the Cabinet.

On 22 March the Cabinet met to consider the health charges. Morrison was in the chair, as Attlee had gone into hospital the previous day. The vast majority of the Cabinet supported Gaitskell's proposals. Bevan objected strongly. He pointed out that the savings involved would be only £23 million out of a total budget of £3,000 million. He asked why could the savings not come from the military estimates? Bevan had a good point for the savings were small, and the rearmament programme was unnecessarily large, reversing a trend away from military expenditure towards health and social insurance. In 1946 Britain had spent £1,653 million on defence, and £334 million on health and insurance; by 1949 these figures were £741 million and £806 million; in 1951 the figures were to be £1,110 million and £810 million. Bevan told the Cabinet he could no longer continue to be a member if it accepted the health charges; Gaitskell countered by demanding unequivocal support.

On 9 April the Cabinet met again; the budget was the following day. Gaitskell replied to Bevan's case by arguing that if he could save £23 million elsewhere he would rather spend it on increased family allowances and old age pensions; he stuck to the health charges, offering to resign if necessary. At this point the Chief Whip visited Attlee in hospital, Attlee supported Gaitskell, though expressing a hope that there would be no splits, which he claimed would be electoral folly. Later in the day the Cabinet took the sole formal vote on a major issue in the whole life of the 1945-1951 governments. Only Bevan and Wilson opposed the cuts, though George Tomlinson, the Minister of Education, supported delay.[17]

There followed a short period of uncertainty as to whether Bevan and Wilson would resign, until later in April Bevan, Wilson, and John Freeman, the Financial Under Secretary at the War Office, announced their resignations. Strachey considered resigning, telling Attlee that he opposed the health charges, but did not consider the issue important enough for resignation (judgement was never one of Strachey's strong points). Labour had experienced its first serious governmental split since 1945.[18]

Attlee subsequently criticised Morrison for losing Bevan. Certainly Morrison made no effort to take a conciliatory line. He had long been a critic of NHS expenditure, and there was no love lost between him and Bevan; once Bevan was asked if he had described Morrison as a third-rate Tammany Hall boss — he replied no, he had described him as a fifth-rate one! Nevertheless, compromise was probably impossible. Gaitskell and others had decided on the cuts. Bevan was unwilling to accept them, and on this occasion his judgement served him well. In 1956 the Guillebaud Committee showed that the earlier increase in NHS spending was small in real terms, and there was no evidence to support claims of extravagance. Bevan was not to know this in 1951, but he was right to see that an allegedly socialist party which could make minute savings on health, while undertaking massive expenditures on defence, was losing sight of its priorities. Gaitskell's main defence is that his cuts were made with an eye to American opinion, but this does not seem to have been a major factor in his decision. Even Dalton criticised Gaitskell in his diary for not thinking enough of the party, and Gaitskell was a protégé of Dalton's! Bevan undoubtedly did not present his case as well as he might have. However, Bevan, for all his failings in this sphere, and more generally in detailed administration and policy, correctly saw the basic requirements of a parliamentary socialist policy. If there was a real villain in the affair it was Gaitskell, and behind him a growing Labour tendency to lose sight of any inspiring conception of socialism. This latter development did not augur well for Labour's future.

Part Three: Legislation and Reform

1950-1951 saw the enactment of no major new piece of legislation. Labour's initial fears about the size of its Parliamentary majority, its belief that the Lords would veto controversial legislation, and divisions within the party over policy meant that the legislative programme was modest compared to 1945-1950.

Minor pieces of legislation covered issues like river pollution, the restoration of land devastated by ironstone pollution, industry in development areas, and other useful, if hardly radical, reforms.

The list of Labour measures introduced during 1950-1951 also includes a Festival of Britain (Sunday Opening) Bill, and Festival of Britain (Additional Loans) Bill, reminders that in May 1951 there opened a great national extravaganza on London's south bank, commemorating the 1851 exhibition, and Britain's more recent achievements. The original idea for the Festival came from the editor of the *News Chronicle* as early as September 1945. The proposal quickly caught on, especially among Labour politicians such as Morrison, who saw that Labour might gain some advantage from such national celebrations. Morrison, ever ready to promote his native London and Labour's electoral fortunes, rapidly became known as 'Lord Festival'. However, as Noel Coward sang at the time in his *Don't Make Fun of the Fair*, 'If no overseas trade appears, we'll have to work for a thousand years, to pay for the Festival of Britain.' Although large numbers of people visited the south bank site, it is doubtful whether the Festival served Labour any useful electoral purpose in the election which took place in October 1951; the result was determined by more long term, and serious, factors.

Chapter Ten

THE 1951 GENERAL ELECTION

'In spite of the fact that we have issued two manifestos within the last two years dealing with aims and objects, it still remains true, I think that we very largely exhausted for the time being our facility for policy formulation in our 1945 Parliament.'

J. Reeves memorandum on 'The Future Policy of the Labour Party'. NEC Minutes, December 1951.

Part One: The Background, Campaign and Results

On 19 September 1951 Attlee announced in a brief statement over the radio that he had asked the King to dissolve Parliament. Britain would go to the polls for the second time within two years on 25 October. Attlee's announcement was widely taken to mark the beginning of the end of six years of Labour government. Opinion polls, which had gained in respectability after their 1950 prediction, had given Labour a small, but steady lead during 1950. By February 1951 Gallup found a 13 per cent Conservative lead, and in September the Conservatives still had a 10 per cent lead.[1]

So why did Attlee call an election in the autumn of 1951? Some supported delay. The opinion polls were ominous. More concretely, some like Morrison saw no contradiction between holding on and their consolidationist position. There were also hopes that the economic situation would improve with the passing of time, and fears that a Conservative government might benefit from many of Labour's reforms and sacrifices. Most of the leadership favoured an autumn election. Many pointed to Labour's small Parliamentary majority, and divisions over policy. Six years of office, together with the especially strenuous Parliamentary demands of 1950-1951, had left a large number of MPs without ideas and physically tired. People like Dalton almost welcomed a rest and period in opposition.

It was even argued that this would help Labour. The Conservatives would have to face the economic problems which were increasingly afflicting Labour. Meanwhile, Labour could heal its wounds and prepare a new programme. Attlee wanted an election before the King left for a long tour of Australia; constitutionalism and love of the monarchy ran deep in this quintessentially conventional man. Therefore on 19 September 1951 Attlee announced that the country would go to the polls in October.[2]

Labour entered the campaign with an even more moderate programme than in 1950. The 1950 result had been interpreted by both the moderates and the left as proving their case concerning electoral strategy. The left argued that a more radical appeal, a more class-based appeal would have aroused enthusiasm and rallied support (at the same time, it challenged a purely electoral conception of programme, arguing that Labour was a party of ideals, not power for power's sake). The moderates pointed to the need to appeal to the middle class, and to the evidence that radical policies were electorally unpopular.[3] The moderates retained a clear advantage. They still dominated the major offices and organs of the party and unions; and most evidence from party officials and opinion polls favoured the consolidationist approach.

In a memorandum to the NEC in March 1950 Morrison attacked the nationalisation shopping list, claiming that it had lost votes; he pushed for a concentration on improving the existing public sector. This ran into strong opposition. However, Morrison found powerful allies, notably when the TUC representatives at the Policy and Publicity Sub Committee meeting in July 1950 came out against further nationalisation, although accepting the possibility of ventures in 'competitive' public enterprise. The moderates were also in a majority on the NEC, and later in July it approved a Morrisonian compromise which promised to consider nationalisation for existing enterprises where they could be shown to be working against the national interest. Although this could be interpreted as leaving the way open for further nationalisation, it avoided any specific commitments.

This compromise was incorporated in a new policy statement entitled *Labour and the New Society*, which was approved at the July 1950 NEC meeting. This proposed three tests for further nationalisation. First, whether the economic life and welfare of the country depended on an industry, and whether it could safely be left in private hands. Secondly, efficiency. And thirdly, there was the test of whether an industry was a monopoly. The statement also promised competitive public enterprise. This programme was subsequently approved by the 1950 Labour conference, which had reverted to an October date in 1950 (it had changed to a Whitsun date in 1937, mainly to avoid following the TUC and appearing a rubber stamp). Predictably, with another general election imminent, delegates showed little desire for public disunity.

The 1951 Labour election manifesto was notable for the fact that it did not contain the word socialist, or socialism. The 1945 manifesto had said that Labour was socialist and 'proud of it'; in 1950 the manifesto stated that Labour was working towards socialism. In 1951 Labour was more evasive, the first time its manifesto had not stated the party was socialist since 1923.

Labour's manifesto stressed four main tasks for the nation: 'to secure peace; to maintain full employment and increase production; to bring down the cost of living; to build a just society'. The manifesto stressed Labour's commitment to greater equality. It argued that in inter-war Britain 39 per cent of the nation's wealth went to personal income after taxation, and 34 per cent to rent, interest and profit; in the 'new' Britain the figures were 48 and 25 per cent respectively, though the manifesto conceded that there was much still to do in this field. The manifesto was essentially an appeal to return Labour to office so that it could consolidate its reforms, preserve full employment, and move further along the path to social justice.

Labour's campaign very much reflected this manifesto. Nationalisation hardly figured as an issue. It was essentially consolidationist and moderate. One notable development during the campaign was foreign policy, which attracted increasing attention, especially developments over the Anglo-Iranian oil dispute. Labour tried hard to develop the warmonger theme, claiming that the Conservatives remained die-hard gunboat imperialists. A second major development was the social welfare issue. On 13 October 1951 B. Seebohn Rowntree and G.R. Lavers's *Poverty and the Welfare State* was published, which demonstrated that there had been a massive reduction in poverty in York since 1936. Labour made great play of this in the closing stages of the campaign. For example, the *Tribune* on 19 October featured Rowntree and Lavers's claim that in 1936 31.1 per cent were below the poverty line, whereas in 1950 the figure was 2.8 per cent; even if unemployment had been the same in 1950 the figure would have been only 7.9 per cent. Put another way, Rowntree and Lavers calculated that if welfare provisions in 1950 were the same as in 1936, the number in poverty would have been 22.2 per cent. Labour claimed that this proved the worth of the welfare state, though the truth of the matter was more complicated. Some of the changes had taken place before 1945; and it is not clear to what extent subsequent changes stemmed from specifically Labour policies. Moreover, the extent of the redistribution of income that had taken place since 1938 was not as great as many thought; the exact change is difficult to assess because of methodological problems, but many poor and rich remained.[4] Nevertheless, at the time the Rowntree and Lavers report, and social welfare in general, provided Labour with excellent campaign material.

Between the 1950 election and the announcement of the 1951 election, the Conservatives produced no new general policy statement, although one appeared during the campaign. This was little more than an expanded version of the Tory manifesto. The main difference compared to the 1950 manifesto on the domestic front was a promise to build 300,000 homes a year. There was further a promise of a short-term excess profits tax to prevent profiteering in the rearmament boom. Foreign policy in general also figured more prominently. For the remainder, the manifesto was again an attack on Labour's claims to being responsible for full employment. It claimed that the Conservatives would preserve the social reforms like the NHS, but would set the people free from controls and continued rationing. The Conservatives would produce a more prosperous Britain!

The Conservative campaign closely mirrored the manifesto. The campaign was nicely summed up by Eden in the Conservatives' first ever television broadcast, as incentive and opportunity at home, peace and security abroad.[5] However, the campaign had a new dimension in its attacks on Labour divisions, particularly on Bevan and his policies. Charles Hill, a Conservative MP, former Radio Doctor, and Bevan's antagonist at the BMA, in his broadcast for the Conservatives popularised the aphorism, 'As one wag put it — "The End Is Nye" '. The Conservatives also sought to undermine Labour's use of the Rowntree-Lavers study by arguing that most of the changes took place before 1945, a misleading claim in that it begged many questions about the extent to which a post-war Conservative government would have maintained and consolidated these gains, though the claim has been repeated by many subsequent critics.[6] At the same time, extensive social security benefits, and the belief in prosperity, provided the basis for new myths about 'scroungers' and wastage. Finally, Labour's warmonger theme was countered by the charge that Labour had grossly mishandled the Iranian crisis.

The smaller parties played no significant part in the election. The Liberals were ideologically and financially bankrupt; they could put forward only 109 candidates (compared to the Conservatives' and Labour's 617 each). The communist position was even more isolated and extreme after the outbreak of the Korean war; the party clearly realised this and put up only 10 candidates.

The result of the election in terms of seats was a narrow Conservative victory, but Labour polled more votes. The Conservatives won 321 seats and 48.0 per cent of the poll, compared to 298 seats and 43.5 per cent in 1950. Labour won 295 seats and 48.8 per cent, against 315 and 46.1 per cent in 1950. So Labour had not only won more votes than the Conservatives, it had also polled more than its winning total in 1950 — and 1945, when it had gained 48.0 per cent. The Liberals' representation dropped from 9 seats to 6, and their vote from 9.1 per cent to 2.6 per cent. The communists again won no seats, and polled a mere 0.1 per cent of the vote, compared to 0.3 per cent in 1950. The result of the election therefore confirmed the demise of the minor parties; the Conservatives and Labour had polled 96.8 per cent between them, the high point of the British two-party system. Turnout at 82.6 per cent was 1.3 per cent lower than in 1950. The swing to the Conservatives was 0.9 per cent, and the Conservatives were left with a majority of 16 seats.[7]

Part Two: Analysis of the Results

The swing was a very low one, and Gallup polls indicated that the vast majority of voters — over 80 per cent — voted the same way as in 1950. So why did the pendulum swing against Labour?

Again, the 1951 result must be seen against a background of events since the previous election, and beyond.

In the period between the 1950 election and the announcement of the 1951 election Labour suffered large defections. The crucial period came in late 1950 and early 1951: in October Labour led the Conservatives in Gallup polls by an average of 46-44 per cent; by January the Conservatives led Labour by 51-38 per cent. Opinion polls showed several interesting factors concerning this change. It coincided with sharply rising prices and a growing concern with the cost of living. The cost of living influenced working-class people considerably. Gallup found that Labour had lost most support among the 'lower income' group. 50 per cent of the group supported Labour in October, but only 38 per cent in January. From this point until the announcement of the election the Conservatives maintained a massive lead. The cost of living remained by far the most widely mentioned issue, reaching 56 per cent in August 1951.

During this period there were other issues which may have harmed Labour, notably the decision to go ahead with iron and steel nationalisation, and the Bevanite split. In January 1951 a poll found that only 24 per cent approved of the nationalisation, compared to 54 per cent who disapproved. In October 1951 a poll found that 51 per cent believed that the Bevanite split had harmed the party, compared to 8 per cent who thought it had helped. However, the polls in general provide little evidence for Dalton's view that the split 'greatly helped' in Labour's defeat, nor is there any strong evidence for the belief that nationalisation was a major issue.[8]

A final point concerning the period 1950-1951 is that during this time Labour looked carefully at its organisation, strengthening its force of agents and deciding to concentrate especially on marginal constituencies.

As in 1945 and 1950, during the campaign itself polls showed a dramatic movement back towards the government. Two general points stand out about this campaign.

The first concerns the role of the media. An innovation was made in the use of three fifteen-minute television party political broadcasts. However, these reached less than 10 per cent of the electorate, and there is little evidence that they, or the radio broadcasts, made any major impact. Similarly, the press lined up in a similar fashion to 1950, and mainly tended to reinforce issues, though over the warmongering issue they helped set the agenda of debate.

A second point concerns the manifestos and campaign. The Conservatives' appeal was undoubtedly more in line with what polls revealed as people's main concerns. Polls on domestic policy showed that the cost of living was easily the most mentioned topic, with 42 per cent thinking it the vital issue in October 1951, compared to 17 per cent in 1950; housing came second with 13 per cent compared to 27 per cent. This meant that the Conservatives' emphasis on these issues struck a more ready chord than Labour's boasts of having achieved full employment, and created the welfare state. However, Labour may have gained some advantage from foreign policy, though it is an exaggeration to claim, as Miliband has done, that without this issue Labour would 'have fared much worse'.[9]

The electoral system also has to be considered. In general it turned 48.0 per cent of the vote for the Conservatives into 52 per cent of the seats, a reasonably proportional result if it is forgotten that Labour won more votes. As in 1950, there was a general bias to the Conservatives worth about 500,000 votes. The postal vote further helped the Conservatives, with a large rise in the number of such votes. The slight drop in turnout probably helped the Conservatives, though the figure of 82.5

per cent on an old register, with few minor party candidates, and in bad weather, is a remarkable testimony to the willingness of the electorate to vote. The vast drop in the number of Liberal candidates had a more serious effect. The turnout and opinion polls indicate that Liberal voters without a candidate of their own did vote on the whole, and they voted around two to one for the Conservatives.

How can the election be summed up compared to 1945 and 1950 in terms of the social composition of the vote, and views of the electorate?

Socially, Labour remained strong among the young, though the Conservatives were making inroads into this group. Labour remained strong among men, though women were increasingly voting Labour. Labour's middle-class vote stayed similar to 1950, and its working-class vote grew. Indeed, in 1951 Labour polled more working-class votes than ever before or since. However, although Z. Bauman has argued that during this whole period there was emerging a unified working class,[10] in a sense it would be wrong to see 1951 as the peak of class-determined voting. Whereas in 1950 Labour suffered few working-class defections, in 1951 polls indicated that some former working-class Labour voters switched to the Conservatives: class was beginning to decline as an electoral factor.

As far as the views of the electorate are concerned, there seems little doubt that these defections reflect a failure to build and sustain a socialist electorate. Indeed, in many ways Labour's policies helped build an increasingly non-socialist electorate.

Labour had not won in 1945 because of mass radicalism, but there is no doubt that its subtle blend of ethicalism, socialist mythology and practical reforms had inspired those who sought both messianic fervour and technocratic solutions. Increasingly after 1945, though the trend had begun before, the ethicalism, the mythology disappeared; technocracy emerged as Labour's central plank. Socialism, as the Fabians proclaimed long before, meant rationality, efficiency, the rule of experts. In 1945, when Labour had never held majority office, this seemed a reasonable promise, if somewhat soulless. After the problems Labour faced during 1945-1951 it seemed a less appealing line. Labour's technocratic appeal, and more generally its class appeal, differed significantly from the old religious appeals of nineteenth-century politics, and the quasi-religious appeal of socialist myth. Voting Labour was an expression of interest as well as — even more than — emotion or allegiance. Labour's class appeal was not some quasi-mystical bond, and it was certainly no reflection of widespread socialist views. It expressed a belief that 'we' would do better under Labour, that it was the party of 'us'. Labour's failure to satisfy some working-class and many middle-class material aspirations proved fatal to its popularity.

At the same time, Labour's emphasis on freedom had always contained an element of tension. In part Labour spoke in the traditional 'negative' sense, referring to freedom from restraint; but Labour's freedom also encompassed a 'positive' element, a commitment to increase people's freedom actually to do things.[11] The 'positive' aspect was a major defence of increasing state activity, but the tension in Labour thinking, and the more traditional 'negative' sense of the word, made it easy for Conservatives to attack Labour on this score. Undoubtedly polls showed a growing concern with what was seen as a loss of liberty. However, it is important not to overstate this aspect, as some have tended to.[12] The appeal of the Conservatives' promise to set the people free was more to affluence than to abstract principle, to the ('negative') freedom to earn more money and be taxed less!

In 1951 the electorate wanted to conserve the gains it had made since the 1930s, and was narrowly divided over whether a 'socialist' Tory Party would do this better than a 'conservative' Labour Party. This is not to say that all voters were rational and fully informed, or that there were not radical socialists, or others on the right who rejected the growth of government expenditure, and mixed market interventionism soon to be known as Butskellism (a term coined from the names of the Labour Chancellor of the Exchequer in 1951, Gaitskell, and his Tory successor, Butler).[13] The point is more that by 1951 the two major parties were appealing increasingly along similar lines of interest, to the ideology of affluence and prosperity, even if in Labour's case there were some egalitarian linkages. Both parties retained some of their more emotive aspects, but they were becoming less prominent than in earlier times. Affluence and prosperity were becoming the central rallying cries, rather than the community of socialism or nation.

It was a change which boded ill for Labour. Electorally, it meant that after 1951 Labour was most likely to return to office after the Conservatives had failed to satisfy expectations, which would probably mean during or after an economic crisis. Ideologically, it marked a development that was likely to reinforce values like greed and inter-personal comparisons that were not conducive to socialism.

In the years immediately after 1951 the debates over the record of the 1945-1951 governments, and the defeat of 1951, were to produce schisms as serious as at any time in the party's history. Over a generation later these debates are still continuing.

Chapter Eleven

CONCLUSION

*'Occasionally late at night at a Labour Party
conference — or in the small hours of the morning
at the more strenuous gatherings of the T.U.C. —
the cry can be heard. "Where", a plaintive maudlin
voice will ask, "did it go wrong?"'*

A. Howard, 'We Are the Masters Now' in M.
Sissons and P. French (editors), *The Age of
Austerity* (1963), p. 15.

Part One: The Realities

The 1945-1951 governments were undoubtedly among the most reformist
in British history, arguably the most reformist. Certainly in terms of major
bills they stand comparison with the second world war coalition, the
1905-1914 Liberal ministry, and Disraeli and Gladstone's ministries of
the 1860s and 1870s. There can also be no doubt that the period provides
a classic example of a programmatic party in power. In *Let Us Face the
Future* Labour promised an extensive programme of reform; by 1951
all the major proposals of this manifesto were enacted (though it could
be argued that some major promises, for example over housing, were
not kept, and many aspirations were not fulfilled).

However, the record of the governments in more ideological terms is
in many ways ambiguous. *Let Us Face the Future* stated that Labour's
goal was the creation of the 'Socialist Commonwealth of Great Britain',
though conceding that this could not come overnight. Were the 1945-
1951 governments socialist? Clearly much depends on how socialism
is defined. Socialism is an eclectic doctrine, encompassing radically different views of the ideal sought, the means of the transition to this ideal,
and immediate policy in a capitalist state.[1] There is no question that on,
say, a revolutionary definition, the 1945-1951 governments were not socialist. Nevertheless, even on more gradualist and moderate definitions of
socialism problems remain in categorising the governments. This can be

seen by reconsidering some of the main elements of the governments' policy, and the changing nature of Labour's electoral politics during this period.

The two main aspects of domestic legislation and reform were the nationalisation programme and social welfare, though it is important to remember that the governments introduced many other useful measures in this general area.

Labour's welfare legislation considerably extended the pre-war services, but much of it had been anticipated by wartime coalition planning. Although it is wrong to think that a Conservative government would necessarily have implemented such plans, it is doubtful in this field if a Conservative government would have pursued a significantly different policy to Labour. Probably the main field where Labour was more radical was health, but the NHS system introduced in 1948 contained many problems, notably the existence side by side of a state and private sector. By 1951 the government was trying to cut back expenditure in this field, and preparing the way for a vision of private affluence and public squalor. Poverty was unquestionably reduced, and many people, especially in the working class, experienced real increases in living standards. There were clear signs of the emergence of an affluent working class, and of a more atomised and complex class structure. Nevertheless, overall the governments' tax and welfare policies were only mildly redistributive, and many very poor people remained — together with many rich.

The nationalisation programme took up considerable Parliamentary time; the iron and steel bill was an especially controversial one. By 1951 ten per cent of the workforce were in the nationalised industries. However, the industries nationalised were either derelict, or public service industries; even iron and steel was a dubious asset commercially. This meant that nationalisation was quickly identified with loss-making and inefficiency; social arguments in favour of maintaining loss-making plant, of keeping prices down, tended to be obscured. Moreover, the public corporation form of nationalisation took no account of the various arguments for common ownership in terms of workers' control. The workers in the nationalised industries may even have become financially worse off in the sense that in times of economic trouble public expenditure becomes a sensitive issue, and the government tries to make economies; certainly in the late 1940s Labour was able to implement its wages policy most effectively in the public sector. Investment cuts for similar reasons posed more long-term problems. Overall, Labour's nationalisation programme involved no clear gradualist strategy. It reflected a Fabian piecemeal optimism, an approach reinforced by demands from powerful trade unions for specific pieces of nationalisation.

The most obvious economic change between pre-war and post-war Britain was full employment, a change which had a major effect in reducing poverty and raising living standards. But it is doubtful whether the governments' policies had much to do with this. A massive post-war cyclical boom was almost certainly more important than the governments' efforts at planning and Keynesian demand management. Indeed, by the late 1940s physical planning was taking a less and less important role in economic policy. The governments' planning even in the early days had never seriously challenged the power of private enterprise in many fields; and the governments' planning agencies and ministries were often staffed by industrialists. Cooperation rather than coercion was the order of the day. This cooperation extended to trade unions as well, and there was an increasing tendency to sponsor quasi-corporatist bodies, including government, management and union representatives. However, it is also important to remember that the economy at this time became more and more part of a world economy, dominated by multi-national corporations, and partially dependent on America for aid. There was certainly no autarchic corporatist economy, or even an approximation to one. The state's peacetime role increased, and the governments were successful in persuading management and unions to pursue some of their desires, for example wage and dividend control in the late 1940s. Nevertheless, by 1951 the government was experiencing serious difficulties in these same spheres, and it had all along had troubles in other areas, such as investment policy and the export of capital. Overall, the structure of British industry remained in many ways similar to the pre-war world, though there was some structural change, and investment and productivity in general rose. Even so, this provided Britain with a fragile economic base in view of the assets which she had sold off, and debts she had incurred, during the war.

The importance of the external dimension is reinforced by a consideration of foreign, defence and colonial policy. Labour's policy during 1945-1951 differed significantly from what had traditionally been seen as a socialist foreign policy. But any judgement of both Labour domestic and foreign policies must take into account the fact that the governments were not entirely free agents. 1945-1951 saw the British government increasingly adopting a position similar to that of the United States. The need for economic aid and fears of Soviet expansionism pressed Britain into a leading role in dividing east from west. Foreign policy also reflected the gulf which existed between the Labour leadership's conception of socialism and that of Soviet communism. However, it would be wrong to think that economic necessity, or fear of the Soviet Union, were the only factors motivating Labour's policy. The defence cuts in the governments' early days, the initial hopes that the UN would assume a major role, the giving up of Empire in India — these and other policies all reflected strong idealistic aspects.

Nevertheless, during 1945-1951 there can be no doubt that Labour's presentation of socialism took on a less idealistic tone, though this was a tendency which had begun well before 1945. In 1945 Labour had proclaimed in its manifesto that it was socialist, and 'proud' of it; in 1951 it was more evasive. By the late 1940s its ethical side had virtually disappeared, it began to stress more efficiency and prosperity — problematic issues in view of its record in some spheres, and the fact that they were issues on which other parties were well equipped to fight. At the same time, Labour's emergence as a natural party of government strengthened the hand of moderates in the party who argued that radicalism would lose support. Labour more and more during 1945-1951 took on the aspect of a brokerage rather than programmatic party. This tendency was further encouraged by the unions; from the outset they had tended to be less programmatic than the socialists, and 1945-1951 saw the enactment of many of their desires. Nevertheless, a strong radical element remained in the party, an element which became increasingly hostile to these tendencies.

Part Two: The Myths

The ambiguities in the Labour governments' record, and varying conceptions of socialism, have lent themselves to radically differing interpretations of this period. Much of this debate has been based on a misreading of the evidence, or has been part of a wider attempt to engage in political myth making.

Many have seen Attlee's government as an extension of the wartime coalition. Paul Addison has written that these ministries 'completed and consolidated the work of the Coalition by establishing a peacetime managed economy, and expanded the welfare state envisaged by Beveridge'.[2]

In many fields Labour clearly pursued policies that had been developed during coalition days. Nevertheless, it is important to remember that Labour helped provide the climate in which these ideas became acceptable, and that Labour ministers were often responsible during the war for the production of post-war planning. Subsequently, the changes in Conservative policy during 1945-1951 owed much to Labour's victory in 1945; it should not be thought that the Conservative Party in 1945 had fully accepted a major role for the state in managing the economy and financing a welfare state. Moreover, it is important to consider the wider vision into which policies fitted. Even among Conservatives who supported, say, a National Health Service there was a tendency to see it in different terms to the way in which Labour supporters saw it. A Conservative might have seen it in terms of providing a 'civilised framework' for capitalist society, even as providing a healthier and more contented workforce. He would also almost certainly have supported the continuation of private medicine, talking in terms of freedom of choice. Support for private practice in the Labour Party was far less strong; the dangers of a two-standard system, and the offensiveness of allowing people to buy what was seen as a right, made many Labour supporters advocates of a total state system. The fact that Labour introduced a dual system reflected the activities of a powerful group, namely the BMA, rather than any basic support for the idea from Bevan. Labour supporters of a National Health Service talked more of an individual's right in relation to the state, advocating a more positive conception of freedom in which the possession of money would play no part.

Similar points could be made for many other policies. Indeed, it is important not to overstate the level of consensus in British politics, either during the war, or after. Considerable ideological differences remained, both between and within the parties. Within the Conservative Party there continued to exist a strong tension between the party's collectivist and libertarian elements. R.A. Butler, Harold Macmillan and others helped commit the Conservative Party to a more interventionist and welfare-orientated policy. But for Angela Thirkell, doyenne conservative novelist of a dying country gentry, 1945 marked, in the words of a 1946 novel, the beginning of the 'brave and revolting new world'. Evelyn Waugh was later to describe Britain at this time as a country under enemy occupation. These views found a strong echo in the backwoods of the Conservative Party, both inside and out of Parliament. Within the Labour Party there were similarly diverse views — a fact which can be seen by considering the debate within the Labour Party after 1951 about the nature of the 1945-1951 governments.

Initially, within some moderate circles of the Labour Party there was little serious discussion of what Labour had achieved, or of its future policy. Among the union leadership in particular there was a tendency to adopt this approach.[3] Many were complacent, believing that Labour's record was impressive, especially in view of the economic troubles the governments faced. It was widely believed that the Conservatives would soon destroy the welfare state, that unemployment would return, and Labour would be swept back into office. Dalton was one of the many who held such views, who almost welcomed defeat in 1951 so that Labour could have a short period in opposition to produce a new programme. After Labour's defeat in the 1955 general election, and especially after its defeat in the 1959 election, this complacency diminished, but the consolidationists of the late 1940s, such as Morrison, failed to produce a satisfactory analysis of what Labour had achieved, or what should be featured in its next programme. Morrison, in a famous aphorism, described socialism as what Labour governments do. Traditionalists like Morrison remained committed to the old dogmas of the party, especially Clause IV, but in reality their radical days were over. They remained rooted in the reforms of 1945-1951; socialism was what the Labour Party had done.[4]

Other moderates saw the need for a more critical examination, and a restatement of Labour policy in the light of this reappraisal. The leading theorist of this group was Anthony Crosland, though his ideas were anticipated by writers such as Durbin and Jay. In Crosland's seminal book *The Future of Socialism*, first published in 1956, he argued that 'The need for a restatement of doctrine is hardly surprising. The old doctrines did not spring from a vacuum, or from acts of pure cerebration in a monastery cell. Each was a product of a particular kind of society.'[5]

Crosland believed that the situation had changed radically since the late 1930s. In 1939 he believed that Britain was essentially an 'unreconstructed capitalist society', but that subsequently a system of 'statism' had emerged. This had been achieved for four main reasons. First, the state had taken on political authority; authority no longer rested with the business class, as the state through various controls could broadly impose its will. Secondly, he argued that there had been a transfer of power from management to labour. Thirdly, there had been a shift of control within capitalism from owners to managers, a change accompanied by a psychological revolution which had humanised management, and made it more socially aware. Finally, there were the achievements of the 1945-1951 Labour governments in creating the welfare state, full employment, and promoting greater equality.[6]

Crosland and the revisionists put great emphasis on these final aspects, especially equality which they identified as the central element in socialism. As such, nationalisation was only a means — not an end — a view that led to a bitter struggle after 1959 when many revisionists sought to amend the part of Clause IV of the party constitution which deals with common ownership. The revisionists believed that considerable progress had been made towards socialism, and that further progress could be pursued through the mixed market, and through government policies such as educational reform. Keynesianism now meant that capitalism could be made stable, even that it could achieve high levels of growth. A prosperous capitalism would produce a high tax revenue, which could finance social reform and social welfare policies.

One major problem here was that the revisionists' defence of the mixed market was based on the assumption that the predominantly private market would continue to prosper in spite of the state using tax and social expenditure to interfere with profit and incentives. To some extent the private sector did flourish during 1945-1951. However, this period also showed that strong capitalist values remained in society, that the state had far from full control over the business world, and that many businessmen seemed largely uninfluenced by social responsibility and other 'psychological' changes. Moreover, a growing sector of the British economy was foreign-controlled, or involved foreign operations; the economy was not insulated from foreign pressures and desires. The revisionist case largely ignored this foreign dimension. The revisionists' dismissal of nationalisation also ignored arguments centring on state ownership to provide workers' control – arguments sometimes linked to power, and checks and balances within a political system (the revisionists were greatly influenced by the dangers of total state control after the experience of totalitarian systems in Germany and the Soviet Union). Furthermore, the revisionists were over-optimistic about the extent of redistribution under the 1945-1951 governments, and the achievements of the welfare state. This was in part understandable in view of the evidence available in the mid-1950s; it was the late 1950s before extensive evidence began to emerge of continuing poverty, and that a small number still held great wealth (though the Royal Commission on wealth in the 1970s showed that considerable changes had taken place). Nevertheless, part of the problem was a vagueness in the revisionists' conception of equality, of the welfare state, and more generally of socialism.[7]

Many on the left of the Labour Party were totally hostile to the revisionist critique, but the left failed to produce an effective critique of its own for the 1945-1951 period, and especially of the nature of a future Labour programme and society. During the 1950s the left tended to get bogged down in disputes over foreign policy and defence, particularly unilateral nuclear disarmament; subsequently, the Common Market became the focus of concern. These were important questions, but they tended to divert attention from the field of domestic policy, though these two areas should not be separated completely.

The left of the Labour Party was less cohesive than the revisionists, and its case was often badly argued; it had no theoretical equivalent of Crosland, though Richard Crossman at times aspired to the role. The left was far less complacent about 1945-1951 than the revisionists. Crossman in *New Fabian Essays*, published in 1952, argued that the Attlee governments had merely produced 'welfare capitalism'.[8] He rejected most of the optimistic revisionist claims about social change. The left identified a series of problems revealed by the 1945-1951 government, and implications for future policy. It was held that much of the trouble could be attributed to moderate leadership, an argument that was sometimes linked to the claim that middle-class leadership was the trouble (the revisionists were frequently attacked for being middle-class intellectuals with little contact with the working class). These arguments were deployed in the 1950s by *Tribune* and the growing Bevanite forces, with the obvious implication that Bevan should be leader. More seriously, some pointed to the role of the civil service. Crossman later wrote that 'If in 1931 the MacDonald Government was killed by the aristocratic embrace, in 1951 the Attlee Government quietly expired in the arms of the Whitehall Establishment.'[9] Finally, it was argued that more nationalisation was needed, that Labour during 1945-1951 had been at fault in not accompanying nationalisation with some form of workers' control, that Labour lacked a sense of priorities — in Bevan's famous words to the 1949 conference, 'The language of priorities is the religion of socialism.'

This left critique contained some good points, but was weakened by several factors. Institutionally, the moderates remained dominant in the party. Historically there were weaknesses. The moderation of the leadership during 1945-1951 reflected widespread moderation in the party, unions and electorate; moderation was just as strong among the working class as among the middle class. The criticism of the eulogies by Attlee and others to the 'loyal' civil service raised more important issues, notably civil service reform and the need for clear Labour thinking. Nevertheless, the record of the 1945-1951 governments is largely understandable in terms of the 1945 programme and make-up of the party; if Labour did not achieve more in terms of specific legislation, it was because it did not set out to do so. Theoretically, the left was on firmer ground in stressing that a case could be made for further nationalisation, especially when linked to workers' control. However, it failed to consider fully the implications of such policies on the private sector, though the opposition of some on the left to the Common Market reflected an awareness of the relationship between the external and internal dimensions (and a growing revival of interest in physical controls). More generally, the left was divided and argued its case poorly. Crossman's claim that the inevitable superiority of nationalised industries in communist countries would lead to capitalist instability must have left many unconvinced – as well as prompting questions about the extent to which the left believed in efficiency as a goal, and how its position differed from communism.

The similarity of parts of the Labour left's critique with those of the non-Labour left further helped weaken its case within the Labour Party. Moderates could raise the old communist, or Trotskyite bogy – though it is true that some on the left of the Labour Party had little or nothing in common with the party's central tenets of gradualism and Parliament-arianism. Certainly the general non-Labour left critique of 1945-1951 reveals the gulf which exists between some Marxists and the Labour Party.

Coates has written that 'In essence the Labour Government of 1945-1951 had not created a socialist commonwealth, nor even taken a step in that direction. It had simply created a mixed economy in which the bulk of industry still lay in private hands, and the six years of its rule had only marginally altered the distribution of social power, privilege, wealth, income, opportunity and security.'[10] This is similar to the conclusion of Crossman and others, but the argument goes beyond the Labour left's position in claiming that Labour necessarily could not have achieved socialism. Four main reasons are suggested to justify this. First, the rejec-tion of 'any perspective (invariably Marxist) which asserted the incom-patibility of interests between the bourgeoisie and the proletariat'. Secondly, its gradualism. Thirdly, its belief in Parliamentarianism. And finally, Labour's view that the state is autonomous. These arguments clearly over-lap, but are best considered separately.

It is difficult to see how Labour adopting a more strident class analysis could increase its support electorally (this point does not concern those Marxist critics who reject electoral politics and the need for legitimacy, but there are other Marxists, for example Miliband, who have argued that electoral politics have an important role to play).[11] Certainly the evidence from 1945-1951 does not support such a view. The exception might be if this argument were taken to mean that Labout should stress more the ethical differences between socialism and capitalism. However, this is rather to argue the need for a more moral line, an approach normally rejected by 'scientific' Marxists.

Although many members of the Labour Party would not agree, there seems little doubt that gradualism raises major problems (though the revolutionary views of many Marxists, especially the élite-vanguard (Leninist-Bolshevik) conception of party, raise their own problems, especially about dictatorship).[12] The relatively successful coexistence of state and private sectors during 1945-1951 resulted more from world factors, such as the cyclical boom, and the nature of Labour's policies, rather than from any necessary symbiosis. Nevertheless, it is possible to suggest a gradualist strategy which might overcome these problems. The control of the financial system would be one policy; taking over profitable industries would be another (although running them in a profit-maximising way might be considered state capitalism rather than socialism); full compensation and moderation in taxation and similar policies should help ensure a stable capitalist sector during the transition.

Parliament during 1945-1951 passed every measure sought by Labour with only minor changes. True, Labour sought no highly radical goals, but there seems no specifically Parliamentary reason to think that such policies could not have been passed, though clearly Parliamentary procedure imposes a limit on the number of major bills which can be considered quickly. It is also important not to confuse support for the Parliamentary road with the Parliamentarianism of many of the Labour leaders, such as Morrison, even Bevan. In particular, Parliament may be important in terms of legitimacy and law making, but it is difficult to argue that it serves any serious Bagehotian educative role; it is essentially irrelevant to most people.

Finally, it is important not to overstate the evidence which 1945-1951 provides for the existence of a non-neutral state. The civil service and others did not prevent Labour introducing more radical policies. The businessmen who operated many of Labour's controls were normally honest and able according to Rogow;[13] pressure groups opposed Labour strongly, notably in the case of iron and steel nationalisation, but they did not significantly alter Labour's intentions as proclaimed in *Let Us Face the Future*. Pressure from the BMA and especially the consultants led to the allowing of private practice within the NHS, but here part of the problem was that Labour had no clear policy in 1945.

The general point about these myths is not that they are without an element of truth; the best myths almost invariably relate to some serious argument, or arguments. The point is more that since 1951 much of the discussion of the 1945-1951 Labour governments has been linked to more general arguments about the nature of British politics, and especially Labour and socialist politics. 1945-1951 has become an important case study in what is really a much wider set of arguments. Clearly these wider arguments are important. However, they are often based on a misreading of the realities of 1945-1951.

Certainly in the context of the Labour Party there has been a tendency for supporters to believe in the party's own myths, to see 1945-1951 as an heroic age, which righted the evils of pre-war Conservative society, which laid the foundations, even established the socialist state. There has been a tendency to ignore the problems in Labour's policy, and the ambiguities of the 1945-1951 governments' achievements. What exactly does the Labour Party mean by socialism? What role, if any, has common ownership to play? What is the relationship between gradualism and the private sector? What constraints are imposed by external forces? What is the relationship of the Labour Party to the trade unions? What exactly do the unions seek from the Labour Party? What are the implications of growing hostility to the unions, of the growth of the middle class, of the decline of class consciousness? How can Labour create a socialist electorate — socialist in any sense of the word?

These questions point to three related areas where change is needed in a Labour Party which seeks to pursue the Parliamentary road to Socialism. First, it must produce a new gradualist policy, breaking away from the old Fabian-union programme. It must challenge the centres of private power vital to the economy, such as banking, and use government expenditure to make a more determined attack on inequality. Secondly, Labour must face the taboo issue of relations with the unions. Unions by their very nature tend to be narrow, and concerned with immediate issues. If Labour is to produce a more challenging and inspiring vision of socialism it must persuade union leaders and their members, to take a broader view. Finally, Labour must pay more attention to the presentation of its message, and media bias. Labour operates in a society in which the media in general is not sympathetic; state aid is necessary to finance dissenting views (and access to broadcasting).

In March 1950, in the aftermath of the 1950 general election, Crossman produced a memorandum, which was circulated among the NEC, relating to the creation of a more socialist electorate. He had little to say about the nature of socialism, or any of the other fundamental questions which the 1945-1950 government had raised. Instead, he suggested the re-creation of socialist cycling clubs, along the lines of the popular *Clarion* clubs of the late nineteenth century; by this medium the socialist faith was to be spread. This proposal serves as an excellent epitaph to the quality of much of the debate on the 1945-1951 governments — and the debate within the Labour Party over the achievement of socialism.

NOTES

Notes to Chapter One

1. For further discussion of the often used, but rarely defined, concept of labourism see T. Forester, *The Labour Party and the Working Class* (1976), pp. 31-42, and J. Saville, 'The Ideology of Labourism' in R. Benewick *et al.* (editors), *Knowledge and Belief in Politics* (1973).

2. For an account of the formation of the party see H. Pelling, *The Origins of the Labour Party* (1971). See also R. Moore, *The Emergence of the Labour Party, 1880-1924* (1978).

3. The best short accounts of the SDF's ideas are H. Collins, 'The Marxism of the Social Democratic Federation' in A. Briggs and J. Saville (editors), *Essays in Labour History, 1886-1923* (1973), and E.J. Hobsbawm, 'Hyndman and the SDF' in E.J. Hobsbawm, *Labouring Men* (1974).

4. For a short account of the Fabians see Hobsbawm, 'The Fabians Reconsidered', op. cit. For a more detailed account of this important group see N. and J. Mackenzie, *The First Fabians* (1977).

5. Far less has been written on the ILP than on the SDF and Fabians, perhaps a reflection of the intellectual preference for the rational. Pelling, op. cit., pp. 145-68 offers a sound short account. R.E. Dowse, *Left in the Centre* (1966) is a general history.

6. The best biography of Hardie is K.O. Morgan, *Keir Hardie* (1975). See also F. Reid, 'Keir Hardie's Conversion to Socialism' in Briggs and Saville (editors), op. cit.

7. For a general account of the unions at this time see H.A. Clegg *et al.*, *A History of British Trade Unions since 1889* (1964). See also J. Saville, 'Trade Unions and Free Labour: the Background to the Taff Vale Decision' in A. Briggs and J. Saville (editors), *Essays in Labour History* (1967).

8. P.F. Clarke, *Lancashire and the New Liberalism* (1971), and T. Wilson, *The Downfall of the Liberal Party* (1966).

9. On this last important point see S. Koss, *Nonconformity in Modern British Politics* (1975), pp. 15-37.

10. For an account of the organisational development of Labour see R. McKibbin, *The Evolution of the Labour Party, 1910-1924* (1974); for an analysis of the impact of the 1918 Reform Act see H.C.G. Matthew *et al.*, 'The Franchise Factor in the Rise of the Labour Party', *English Historical Review*, Volume XCI, Number 361 (1976).

11. Clarke, 'Liberals, Labour and the Franchise', *English Historical Review*, Volume XCII, Number 364 (1977). c.f. K.D. Wald, 'Class and the Vote before the First World War', *British Journal of Political Science*, Volume 8, Number 4 (1978).

12. For a discussion of the development of Webb's ideas at this time see J.M. Winter *Socialism and the Impact of War* (1974).

13. R. Miliband, *Parliamentary Socialism* (1973), p. 62.
14. For a discussion of political myths see H. Tudor, *Political Myth* (1972).
15. See R. Barker, 'Political Myth: Ramsay MacDonald and the Labour Party', *History*, Volume 61, Number 201 (1976). For a general life of MacDonald see D. Marquand, *Ramsay MacDonald* (1977).
16. For example, Winter, op. cit., p. 3.
17. S. Beer, *Modern British Politics* (1965), especially p. 126.
18. M. Cowling, *The Impact of Labour* (1971), especially pp. 420-1.
19. In 1918 85.9 per cent of the PLP was union-sponsored; in 1922 the figure was 60.6 per cent; and in 1923 it was 53.4 per cent.
20. Miliband, op. cit., pp. 121-51.
21. D. Coates, *The Labour Party and the Struggle for Socialism* (1975), p. 25.
22. ibid., p. 26.
23. For an account of Labour's economic policy at this time see R. Skidelsky, *Politicians and the Slump* (1967). See also R. McKibbin, 'The Economic Policy of the Second Labour Government, 1929-1931', *Past and Present*, Number 66 (1975).
24. See R. Eatwell and A.W. Wright, 'Labour and the Lessons of 1931', *History*, Volume 63, Number 208 (1978).
25. See B. Pimlott, 'The Socialist League: Intellectuals and the Labour Left in the 1930s', *Journal of Contemporary History*, Volume 6, Number 3 (1972), and P. Seyd, 'Factionalism within the Labour Party: the Socialist League, 1932-1937' in A. Briggs and J. Saville (editors), *Essays in Labour History, 1918-1939* (1977).
26. For an account of Cole's and Laski's views see L.P. Carpenter, *G.D.H. Cole* (1973), and H.A. Deane, *The Political Ideas of Harold J. Laski* (1955).
27. For example, H. Pelling, *A Short History of the Labour Party* (1976), p. 75. Cripps's official biography, C.A. Cooke, *The Life of Richard Stafford Cripps* (1957), also fails adequately to deal with this period.
28. There is no satisfactory biography of Dalton, and his autobiography, although on the whole readable, is unreliable.
29. See B. Donoughue and G.W. Jones, *Herbert Morrison: Portrait of a Politician* (1973).
30. Tawney's life and views are dealt with in R. Terrill, *R.H. Tawney* (1974).
31. There is no adequate biography of Attlee, and his autobiography is elliptical to say the least. Some of his views are considered in W. Golant, 'The Emergence of C.R. Attlee as Leader of the Parliamentary Labour Party in 1935', *Historical Journal*, Volume 13, Number 2, (1970).
32. D. Caute, *The Fellow Travellers* (1973). Some less rational aspects are dealt with in G. Watson, 'Were the Intellectuals Duped?', *Encounter*, December 1973.
33. For an account of Bevin's life and views at this time see A. Bullock, *The Life and Times of Ernest Bevin*, Volume 1 (1960). There is no sound biography of Citrine, and his autobiography says little.
34. For a general, though somewhat unoriginal, account of Labour in the 1930s see B. Pimlott, *Labour and the Left in the 1930s* (1977).
35. A pedestrian survey of Labour's foreign policy at this time may be found in J.F. Naylor, *Labour's International Policy* (1969).
36. A passionate and largely uncritical account of Bevan's life before 1945 may be found in M. Foot, *Aneurin Bevan, 1897-1945* (1962).

37. P. Addison, *The Road to 1945* (1975). See also D. Winch, *Economics and Policy* (1969), pp. 145-218 and 341-51.
38. Strachey's life and views are dealt with a little disappointingly in H. Thomas, *John Strachey* (1973).
39. D. Howell, *British Social Democracy* (1976), p. 53.
40. See Addison, op. cit., and A. Calder, *The People's War* (1969).

Notes to Chapter Two

1. A. Bullock, *The Life and Times of Ernest Bevin*, Volume 2 (1967), pp. 372-7, Donoughue and Jones, op. cit., pp. 333-34, and F. Williams, *A Prime Minister Remembers* (1961), pp. 62-3.
2. For a general account of the election see R.B. McCallum and A. Readman, *The British General Election of 1945* (1947). Another disappointing account may be found in W. Harrington and P. Young, *The 1945 Revolution* (1978).
3. Miliband, op. cit., p. 278.
4. Full details of the result may be found in F.W.S. Craig, *British Parliamentary Election Statistics, 1918-1968* (1970), especially pp. 11-12.
5. For an account of general polling techniques, and problems, see R. Hodder-Williams, *Public Opinion Polls and British Politics* (1970).
6. M. Cole, *The General Election 1945 and After* (1945), p. 24.
7. A.J.P. Taylor, *English History, 1914-1945* (1965), p. 596.
8. For example, A. Marwick, *Britain in the Century of Total War* (1970), especially pp. 259-323.
9. For an account of Cripps's popularity, especially during 1942, see Addison, op. cit., pp. 190-210.
10. For example, see R. Crossman, 'The Lessons of 1945' in P. Anderson and R. Blackburn (editors), *Towards Socialism* (1965). For an account of the Left Book Club see J. Lewis, *The Left Book Club* (1970).
11. For a discussion of propaganda, a term frequently used, but rarely defined, see T.H. Qualter, *Propaganda and Psychological Warfare* (1963).
12. For example, G. Wigg, *George Wigg* (1972), p. 14.
13. A. Marwick, 'Middle Opinion in the Thirties: Planning, Progress and Political "Agreement"', *English Historical Review*, Volume LXXIX, Number 311 (1964).
14. Statistics in this book are taken mainly from B.R. Mitchell and H.G. Jones, *Second Abstract of British Historical Statistics*, (1971).
15. For example, W.S. Churchill, *Triumph and Tragedy* (1954), p. 509.
16. J.D. Hoffman, *The Conservative Party in Opposition, 1945-1951* (1963), especially pp. 26-9.
17. Concern over programme was especially strong after 1945 among Conservatives who sought a more positive policy commitment. See ibid.
18. For a discussion of the effects of the mass media and some comments on the 1945 campaign see C. Seymour Ure, *The Political Impact of the Mass Media* (1973), pp. 15-63 and 202-39.
19. An introductory discussion of voting behaviour in Britain may be found in J. Blondel, *Voters, Parties and Leaders* (1974), pp. 49-87, and P.G.J. Pulzer, *Political Representation and Elections in Britain* (1975). A more detailed, and historical, account may be found in D. Butler and D. Stokes, *Political Change in*

Britain (1975), *passim*.

20. Some of these points are dealt with in J. Bonham, *The Middle Class Vote* (1954).
21. Miliband, op. cit., p. 272, P. Foot, *The Politics of Harold Wilson* (1968), p. 80, and Addison, op. cit., especially p. 164.
22. Coates, op. cit., pp. vii-ix, and p. 42.

Notes to Chapter Three

1. Bullock, *The Life and Times of Ernest Bevin*, Volume 2, pp. 392-3, and Donoughue and Jones, op. cit., pp. 339-43.
2. See Bullock, *The Life and Times of Ernest Bevin*, Volume 2, p. 393, H. Dalton, *High Tide and After* (1962), pp. 8-14, and Donoughue and Jones, op. cit., pp. 344-7. For a complete list of the government see D. Butler and A. Sloman, *British Political Facts, 1900-1975* (1975), pp. 32-6.
3. In 1945 the percentage of trade union-sponsored MPs was the lowest ever — 30.8 per cent, compared to 51.3 per cent in 1935.
4. For an account of the workings of Attlee's Cabinets see H. Daalder, *Cabinet Reform in Britain, 1914-1963* (1964), pp. 99-107, J.P. Mackintosh, *The British Cabinet* (1977), pp. 429-32, and P. Gordon Walker, *The Cabinet* (1972), pp. 35-8 and 162-3.
5. For a discussion of whether or not Britain has seen the emergence of 'Prime Ministerial' government see R.H.S. Crossman, *Inside View* (1971), and A. King (editor), *The British Prime Minister* (1969).
6. Marwick, *Britain in the Century of Total War*, p. 331.
7. Miliband, op. cit., pp. 292-3.
8. For example, A.A. Rogow, *The Labour Government and British Industry, 1945-1951* (1955), p. 4.
9. Even a moderate like Dalton has argued this. Dalton, op. cit., p. 138.
10. A full set of by-election figures may be found in Craig, op. cit., pp. 25-8.
11. Addison, op. cit., p. 273, and Rogow, op. cit., p. 164.
12. Miliband, op. cit., pp. 285-310.
13. See H. Morrison, *Government and Parliament* (1962), pp. 73-244, and K.C. Wheare, *Government by Committee* (1955).
14. R.K. Alderman, 'Discipline in the Parliamentary Labour Party, 1945-1951', *Parliamentary Affairs*, Volume XVIII, Number 3 (1965), and H. Berrington, *Backbench Opinion in the House of Commons, 1945-1955* (1973).
15. Beer, op. cit., especially pp. 105-242, and R.T. McKenzie, *British Political Parties* (1963), especially pp. 297-576. See also H.B. Cole, *The British Labour Party* (1977) and L. Minkin, *The Labour Party Conference* (1978).
16. V.L. Allen, *Trade Unions and the Government* (1960), pp. 263-4.

Notes to Chapter Four

1. There is no sound account of the 1945-1951 government's legislative programme. D.N. Pritt, *The Labour Government, 1945-1951* (1963) is very unreliable (Pritt was expelled from the Labour Party in 1940 for communist sympathies). Howell, op. cit., pp. 135-79, presents a generally sound short account.
2. See Donoughue and Jones, op. cit., especially pp. 348-62.

170   *Notes*

3. See D.N. Chester, *The Nationalisation of British Industry, 1945-1951* (1975). This is the official history of nationalisation; its structure makes it difficult to give brief page references.
4. Rogow, op. cit., pp. 28-9.
5. See Chester, op. cit.
6. For example, R.A. Brady, *Crisis in Britain* (1950), Coates, op. cit., p. 51, Miliband op. cit., p. 279; etc.
7. Marwick, *Britain in the Century of Total War*, p. 336.
8. Coates, op. cit., p. 49.
9. Allen, op. cit., especially p. 272.
10. Miliband, op. cit., pp. 289-90; see also Rogow, op. cit., pp. 104; etc.
11. Miliband, op. cit., p. 288.
12. See Chester, op. cit.
13. See Allen, op. cit., especially pp. 261-4.
14. For a short account of Labour's welfare legislation see D. Fraser, *The Evolution of the Welfare State* (1973), pp. 192-222.
15. For an account of Beveridge's life and views see J. Harris, *William Beveridge* (1977).
16. See K. Coates and R. Silburn, *Poverty: the Forgotten Englishmen* (1975), pp. 185-91.
17. See Addison, op. cit., p. 225, and F. Bealey, *The Social and Political Thought of the British Labour Party* (1970), p. 17.
18. For example, J.C. Kincaid, *Poverty and Equality in Britain* (1977), p. 61.
19. R. Titmuss, 'The Irresponsible Society' in R. Titmuss, *Essays on 'The Welfare State'* (1976), p. 229.
20. For a general account of the formation of the NHS see H. Eckstein, *The English Health Service* (1958), and A.J. Willcocks, *The Creation of the National Health Service* (1967).
21. H. Eckstein, 'The Politics of the British Medical Association', *Political Quarterly*, Volume 26, Number 4 (1955), reprinted in R. Rose (editor), *Studies in British Politics* (1966).
22. Bevan's role is dealt with very sympathetically by M. Foot, *Aneurin Bevan, 1945-1960* (1973), pp. 100-215.
23. See J.B. Cullingworth, *Housing Needs and Planning Policy* (1960), especially pp. 3-71, and N. Rosenberg, *Economic Planning in the Building Industry, 1945-1945* (1960).
24. See Foot, *Aneurin Bevan, 1945-1960*, pp. 57-99.
25. F. Berry, *Housing: the Great British Failure* (1974), pp. 46-7.
26. See W.K. Hancock and M.M. Gowing, *The British War Economy* (1949).
27. The most detailed study of policy during 1945-1951, though somewhat out of date, is G.D.N. Worswick and P.H. Ady (editors), *The British Economy, 1945-1950* (1952). Another detailed account may be found in J.C.R. Dow, *The Management of the British Economy, 1945-1960* (1964), *passim*. A short account is given in S. Pollard, *The Development of the British Economy, 1914-1967* (1976), pp. 357-407.
28. Rogow, op. cit., p. 28.
29. ibid., especially pp. 49-117. For a longer and more theoretical perspective see T. Smith, *The Politics of the Corporate Economy* (1979).

30. Miliband, op. cit., p. 290.

31. T.W. Hutchison, *Economics and Economic Policy in Britain, 1946-1966* (1968), p. 27.

32. Dalton, op. cit., p. 13.

33. R.C.O. Matthews, 'Why Has Britain Had Full Employment since the War', *Economic Journal*, Volume LXXVIII, Number 3 (1968).

34. For an account of the loan negotiations see Dalton, op. cit., pp. 68-89.

35. R.F. Harrod, *The Life of John Maynard Keynes* (1951), pp. 586-623.

36. Foot, *Aneurin Bevan, 1945-1960*, pp. 47-56, and G.D.H. Cole, *A History of the Labour Party from 1914* (1948), p. 464.

37. See Thomas, op. cit., pp. 230-6.

38. Dalton, op. cit., p. 144.

39. There is no sound account of Labour foreign policy during this period. M.A. Fitzsimmons, *The Foreign Policy of the British Government, 1945-1951* (1952) is out of date, narrative, and hardly considers many issues. M.R. Gordon, *Conflict and Consensus in Labour's Foreign Policy, 1914-1965* (1969), especially pp. 102-247, is more up to date and analytical, but rather misleading in its 'socialist' versus 'traditional' perspective.

40. For example, Pritt, op. cit., p. 76.

41. J. Burridge, *British Labour and Hitler's War* (1976), p. 13.

42. R. Barclay, *Ernest Bevin and the Foreign Office, 1932-1969* (1975), p. 43.

43. Burridge, op. cit., *passim*.

44. See Naylor, op. cit., *passim*.

45. For an account of Bevin's foreign policy see A. Schlaim *et at.*, *British Foreign Secretaries since 1945* (1977), pp. 27-69. For an account of the development of general Labour attitudes to Russia see B. Jones, *The Russia Complex* (1978).

46. Miliband, op. cit., p. 295.

47. Foot, *Aneurin Bevan, 1945-1960*, pp. 29-32.

48. For a short account of defence policy see C.J. Bartlett, *The Long Retreat* (1972), pp. 1-77. See also J. Bayliss (editor), *British Defence Policy in a Changing World* (1977).

49. For a discussion of colonial policy see P.S. Gupta, *Imperialism and the British Labour Movement, 1914-1964* (1975), especially pp. 275-348.

50. For example, R. Palme Dutt, *The Crisis in Britain and the British Empire* (1953), *passim*.

Notes to Chapter Five

1. Dalton, op. cit., p. 186.

2. ibid., pp. 203-5.

3. Dow, op. cit., pp. 22-6.

4. For example, A.J. Youngson, *Britain's Economic Growth, 1920-1966* (1968), p. 168.

5. Dalton, op. cit., pp. 238-46.

6. Donoughue and Jones, op. cit., pp. 413-25.

7. Cooke, op. cit., p. 358.

8. Donoughue and Jones, op. cit., pp. 351-4.

9. Dalton, op. cit., pp. 272-86.
10. For example, Calder, op. cit., p. 270.
11. See Cooke, op. cit., pp. 363-404, and D. Marquand, 'Sir Stafford Cripps' in M. Sissons and P. French (editors), *The Age of Austerity* (1963). Neither explains the change of the Cripps of the 1930s into the Cripps of the 1940s.
12. Gordon, op. cit., pp. 131-2.
13. For a short account of this important development see D. Watt, 'Withdrawal from Greece' in Sissons and French (editors), op. cit.
14. For example, Barclay, op. cit., p. 33.
15. For a brief introduction to the cold war debate see P. Seabury, 'Cold War Origins, 1', and B. Thomas, 'Cold War Origins 2', *Journal of Contemporary History*, Volume 3, Number 1 (1968).
16. Gordon, op. cit., p. 103.
17. For an account of the decision to make the atomic bomb see M. Gowing, *Independence and Deterrence*, 2 volumes (1974).
18. Bartlett, op. cit., p. 31.
19. Mackintosh, op. cit., p. 494.
20. See Gupta, op. cit.
21. For example, I. Davies, 'The Labour Commonwealth', *New Left Review*, Number 22 (1963).
22. For an account of Britain's rule in Palestine see C. Sykes, *Crossroads to Israel* (1965), especially pp. 315-438, and J. Cohen, *Palestine: Retreat from the Mandate* (1978).
23. Miliband, op. cit., p. 294.
24. For example, Schlaim *et al.*, op. cit., p. 61, and Dalton, op. cit., p. 148.
25. See Hoffman, op. cit.
26. See Chester, op. cit.
27. Crossman, op. cit., p. 154.
28. See Chester, op. cit.
29. Addison, op. cit., p. 273.
30. For example, Marwick, *Britain in the Century of Total War*, p. 358.
31. For an account of the development of Labour's educational policies see R. Barker, *Education and Politics* (1972), especially pp. 81-97.

Notes to Chapter Six

1. For an account of Strachey's involvement in the groundnuts scheme see Thomas, op. cit., pp. 245-56. A more lighthearted look at rationing may be found in S. Cooper, 'Snoek Piquante' in Sissons and French (editors), op. cit.
2. D. Hughes, 'The Spivs', and J. Gross, 'The Lynskey Tribunal', ibid.
3. For example, Youngson, op. cit., p. 169.
4. Beer, op. cit., p. 200.
5. For a less than sympathetic discussion of Wilson's policy see P. Foot, op. cit., pp. 50-87, and A. Roth, *Sir Harold Wilson: Yorkshire Walter Mitty* (1977), especially pp. 87-137.
6. E. Wigham, *Strikes and the Government, 1893-1974* (1976), pp. 100-105.
7. Hutchison, op. cit., pp. 19-37.

8. A. Shonfield, *British Economic Policy since the War* (1958), p. 168.
9. For example, S. Brittan, *Steering the Economy* (1969), especially pp. 107-12.
10. Donoughue and Jones, op. cit., p. 447.
11. For a brief account of devaluation see Dow, op. cit., pp. 40-5.
12. Pollard, op. cit., p. 362.
13. For example, Hutchison, op. cit., pp. 68-82.
14. Foot, *Aneurin Bevan, 1945-1960*, pp. 227-8.
15. For an account of the emergence of a separate West Germany, and Britain's policy towards Germany, see F.S. Northedge, *British Foreign Policy* (1961), pp. 64-98.
16. For example, Schlaim *et al.*, op. cit., p. 46.
17. F. Williams, *Ernest Bevin* (1952), p. 267.
18. R.N. Rosecranz, 'British Defence Strategy, 1945-1952' in R.N. Rosecranz (editor), *The Dispersion of Nuclear Weapons: Strategy and Politics* (1964), pp. 67-9.
19. For example, Palme Dutt, op. cit., especially p. 323.
20. Gupta, op. cit., p. 347.
21. For a discussion of the troubles over the setting up of the NHS during 1947-1948 see Foot, *Aneurin Bevan, 1945-1960*, pp. 138-215.
22. ibid., p. 190.
23. For example, Addison, op. cit., p. 273.
24. See W.A. Robson, *Local Government in Crisis* (1966), *passim*.
25. See Chester, op. cit., and D. Burn, The Steel Industry.
26. Miliband, op. cit. p. 301.
27. See Hoffman, op. cit., pp. 221-69.
28. See Chester, op. cit.
29. Donoughue and Jones, op. cit., p. 400.
30. Dalton, op. cit., p. 137.
31. For example, G. Hodgson, 'The Steel Debates' in Sissons and French (editors), op. cit., pp. 310-11.
32. Miliband, op. cit., p. 292.
33. P. Bromhead, *The House of Lords and Contemporary Politics* (1958), pp. 157-76.
34. See D. Butler, *The Electoral System in Britain since 1918* (1968), pp. 102-39.

Notes to Chapter Seven

1. For a general account of the election see H.G. Nicholas, *The British General Election of 1950* (1951).
2. See Rogow, op. cit., pp. 167-70.
3. Donoughue and Jones, op. cit., p. 447.
4. ibid., pp. 448-9, and Dalton, op. cit., p. 337.
5. Donoughue and Jones, op. cit., pp. 441-8.
6. Foot, *Aneurin Bevan, 1945-1960*, especially pp. 254-79.
7. E. Eldon Barry, *Nationalisation in British Politics* (1965), p. 378.
8. T.F. Carbery, *Consumers in Politics* (1969), pp. 162-5.
9. Hoffman, op. cit., *passim*.
10. For a more detailed analysis of the results see Craig, op. cit., p. 13.
11. M. Abrams, *British Standards of Living* (1948), especially pp. 9-12.

12. Dalton, op. cit., p. 93.
13. Howell, op. cit., p. 169.
14. Subsequent media studies would tend to bear this out, for example, the coverage of strikes. See Glasgow Media Group, *Bad News* (1976).
15. See Butler, op. cit., pp. 102-39.
16. Nicholas, op. cit., pp. 4 and 9.
17. For example, R. Blake, *The Conservative Party from Peel to Churchill* (1972), p. 263.
18. Beer, op. cit., p. 211.

Notes to Chapter Eight

1. Trade union-sponsored MPs accounted for 30.8 per cent of the PLP in 1945, 34.9 per cent in 1950, and 35.6 per cent in 1951.
2. For example, Schlaim *et al.*, op. cit., p. 31.
3. Miliband, op. cit., p. 298.
4. See C.H. Darke, *The Communist Technique in Britain* (1953), especially p. 130, and J. Goldstein, *The Government of British Trade Unions* (1952), *passim*.
5. For an account of Labour's relations with the unions after 1945 see M. Harrison, *Trade Unions and the Labour Party since 1945* (1960).
6. See Allen, op. cit., pp. 288-9.

Notes on Chapter Nine

1. For example, Williams, *A Prime Minister Remembers*, especially p. 230.
2. Granada Historical Record, *Clem Attlee* (1967), pp. 49 and 55.
3. Dalton, op. cit., p. 360.
4. See Barclay, op. cit., pp. 96-8.
5. For an account of Morrison's period as Foreign Secretary see Schlaim *et al.*, op. cit., pp. 70-80.
6. Donoughue and Jones, op. cit., pp. 479-514.
7. Gordon, op. cit., p. 127.
8. Barclay, op. cit., p. 89.
9. See Foot, *Aneurin Bevan, 1945-1960*, pp. 304-5 and 310.
10. For more detail on colonial policy see Gupta, op. cit., pp. 336-46.
11. Dow, op. cit., p. 55.
12. Rogow, op. cit., p. 34.
13. Dow, op. cit., pp. 35 and 61.
14. Donoughue and Jones, op. cit., pp. 465-6.
15. Foot, *Aneurin Bevan, 1945-1960*, p. 296.
16. Dalton, op. cit., pp. 363-5.
17. Gordon Walker, op. cit., pp. 24 and 135-6.
18. Foot, *Aneurin Bevan, 1945-1960*, pp. 320-9, and Thomas, op. cit., p. 266.

Notes to Chapter Ten

1. For a general account of the election see D.E. Butler, *The British General Election of 1951* (1952).
2. Dalton, op. cit., pp. 376-7, Donoughue and Jones, op. cit., pp. 501-3, and Granada

Historical Record, op. cit., pp. 47-50.

3. Donoughue and Jones, op. cit., pp. 455-69, and Foot, *Aneurin Bevan, 1945-1960*, pp. 280-346.

4. See R. Titmuss, *Income Distribution and Social Change* (1962). See also J. Westergaard and H. Resler, *Class in a Capitalist Society* (1976).

5. For an account of the first television party political broadcasts see G. Wyndham Goldie, *Facing the Nation* (1977), pp. 92-103.

6. For example, Pollard, op. cit., p. 397.

7. For fuller details see Craig, op. cit., p. 14.

8. Dalton, op. cit., p. xiii.

9. Miliband, op. cit., p. 317.

10. Z. Bauman, *Between Class and Elite* (1973), especially p. 231.

11. For a brief discussion of the concepts of freedom see I. Berlin, 'Two Concepts of Liberty' in I. Berlin, *Four Essays on Liberty* (1969), and in A. Quinton (editor), *Political Philosophy* (1967).

12. For example, Blake, op. cit., p. 267.

13. Many economists have argued that the growth of government activity has seen two major upsurges in the twentieth century. These occurred during the first and second world wars. However, recent econometric analysis has played down the importance of the wars, revealing a more steady trend. (See C.V. Brown and P.M. Jackson, *Public Sector Economics* (1978), especially pp. 89-92.) Many economic factors can account for this, but it is part of the argument of this book that Labour's policies helped condition other parties and groups to such activity.

Notes to Chapter Eleven

1. For an introductory discussion of the varieties of socialist thought see G.D.H. Cole, 'What Is Socialism?', *Political Studies*, Volume 1, Numbers 1 and 2 (1953); this is reprinted in A. de Crespigny and J. Cronin (editors), *Ideologies in Politics* (1975). See also P. Sedgwick, 'Varieties of Socialist Thought', *Political Quarterly*, Volume 40, Number 4 (1969); this is reprinted in B. Crick and W. Robson (editors), *Protest and Discontent* (1970). See also R.N. Berki, *Socialism* (1975).

2. Addison, op. cit., p. 273.

3. See Harrison, op. cit., *passim*.

4. See Donoughue and Jones, op. cit., pp. 515-61.

5. C.A.R. Crosland, *The Future of Socialism* (1967), p. 61.

6. For a critical account of Crosland's views on these issues see A. Arblaster, 'Anthony Crosland: Labour's Last "Revisionist"?', *Political Quarterly*, Volume 48, Number 4 (1977).

7. For the argument that the welfare state is almost invariably an imprecise term see R. Titmuss, *Commitment to Welfare* (1968), especially p. 124.

8. R. Crossman, 'Towards a Philosophy of Socialism' in R. Crossman (editor), *New Fabian Essays* (1952), pp. 26-7.

9. Crossman, 'The Lessons of 1945', p. 155.

10. Coates, op. cit., p. 47.

11. See R. Miliband, 'Moving on', in R. Miliband and J. Saville (editors), *The Socialist Register 1976* (1976).

12. See K. Coates, 'How Not to Reappraise the New Left', ibid.

13. Rogow, op. cit., pp. 65-6.

BIBLIOGRAPHICAL ESSAY

This short bibliographical essay does not contain all the books mentioned in references nor other works used, including primary sources. Its main purpose is to list the most useful works for the general reader.

General Histories of the Labour Party

There are several books which deal with the Labour Party over the course of most of its history. H. Pelling, *A Short History of the Labour Party* (1976) is concise, but a little pedestrian. R. Miliband, *Parliamentary Socialism* (1973) is more argumentative, and written from a Marxist viewpoint. This is also true of D. Coates, *The Labour Party and the Struggle for Socialism* (1975), which is less useful as a history, but stronger analytically. D. Howell, *British Social Democracy* (1976) deals mainly with the post-1931 period, but is probably the most useful book.

The Labour Party before 1945

R. Moore, *The Emergence of the Labour Party, 1880-1924* (1978) is a useful introduction. R. Skidelsky, *Politicians and the Slump* (1968) offers a detailed analysis covering the important years 1929-1931. B. Pimlott, *Labour and the Left in the 1930s* (1977) recounts the developments of the immediate pre-war years, though without fully analysing vital questions like the impact of Keynes and the popular front. P. Addison, *The Road to 1945* (1975) tries to show the development of a reforming consensus before 1945; the book is well argued, but it ignores the extent to which radical differences remained.

The Labour Party and Governments, 1945-1951

The general elections of 1945, 1950 and 1951 are covered in the Nuffield election studies, written by R.B. McCallum and A. Readman, H.G. Nicholas, and D. Butler respectively. They tend to be very empirical and narrow, but contain a lot of useful information. A more lively account of the 1945 election may be found in W. Harrington and P. Young, *The 1945 Revolution* (1978). There is no satisfactory general history of the governments. D.N. Pritt, *The Labour Government, 1945-1951* (1963) is very unreliable (the author was expelled from the Labour Party in 1940 for pro-communist sympathies). A rather journalistic set of essays may be found in M. Sissons and P. French (editors), *The Age of Austerity, 1945-1951* (1963). Nationalisation is dealt with in great detail by D.N. Chester, *The Nationalisation of British Industry, 1945-1951* (1975). A shorter presentation may be found in E. Eldon Barry, *Nationalisation in British Politics* (1965). The best short account of Labour's welfare legislation is D. Fraser, *The Evolution of the Welfare State* (1973). For a more detailed account of the creation of the NHS see H. Eckstein, *The English Health Service* (1958). The most detailed account of economic policy at this time, though somewhat out of date, is G.D.N. Worswick and P.H. Ady (editors), *The British Economy, 1945-1950* (1952). See also J.C.R. Dow, *The Management of the British*

Economy, 1945-1960 (1964). Economic policy in relation to industry is covered by A.A. Rogow, *The Labour Government and British Industry, 1945-1951* (1955). The governments' relations with the unions are briefly considered in V.L. Allen, *Trade Unions and the Government* (1960). Labour's relations with the unions are covered in considerable detail in M. Harrison, *Trade Unions and the Labour Party since 1945* (1960). There is no sound account of Labour's foreign policy. Probably the most useful book is M.R. Gordon, *Conflict and Consensus in Labour's Foreign Policy, 1914-1965* (1969). A narrative, but useful account of defence policy may be found in C.J. Bartlett, *The Long Retreat* (1972). Colonial policy is well covered in P.S. Gupta, *Imperialism and the British Labour Movement, 1914-1964* (1975).

Autobiographies and Biographies

There is no satisfactory biography of Attlee, and his autobiography is very unrevealing. Alan Bullock's biography of Bevin only covers the period up to 1945. Morrison's life is analysed in detail and critically in B. Donoughue and G.W. Jones, *Herbert Morrison: Portrait of a Politician* (1973). There is no adequate biography of Dalton. His memoirs are extensive, containing much interesting information, but they must be treated with caution; as Dalton remarks in the introduction, autobiography is an exercise in egotism. Cripps's life similarly awaits a good biographer. C.A. Cooke, *The Life of Richard Stafford Cripps* (1957) is very disappointing. Michael Foot's two volume biography of Bevan is well written and passionate; it is the story of a hero, who fought to retain the soul of the Labour Party.

Other Works

Countless other books could be considered relevant to the 1945-1951 governments especially if the wider implications of the governments are considered. Some of the main debates about the extent to which these years saw major social and economic change can be seen clearly in the debate within the Labour Party after 1951. Two classic works in this context are R. Crossman (editor), *New Fabian Essays* (1952), and C.A.R. Crosland, *The Future of Socialism* (1967), the latter first published in 1956. Part of the discussion surrounding the 1945-1951 governments concerns whether or not they were socialist; the nature of socialism is therefore important. R.N. Berki, *Socialism* (1975) offers a sound introduction to the varieties of socialism. It is also important to remember that 1945-1951 saw important developments in the Conservative Party. For an account of the party during these years see D. Hoffman, *The Conservative Party in Opposition, 1945-1951* (1963). For further statistical information see B.R. Mitchell and H.G. Jones, *Second Abstract of British Historical Statistics* (1971) and D. Butler and A. Sloman, *British Political Facts, 1900-1975* (1975), (nb some statistics in this book are taken from other sources, including primary ones).

INDEX